First published 2026

Published by Milairo Press

An imprint of Milairo LLC

Miami, Florida

milairo.com

ISBN: 979-8-234-04554-6

Printed in the United States of America

The AI-Ready Firm

PART THREE — THE IMPLEMENTATION PLAYBOOK

APPENDIX

Why This Book Exists

In the past three years, artificial intelligence has gone from a curiosity on the edge of the accounting profession to the loudest topic in every conference breakout session, vendor demo, and partner conversation I have had. The promise is real. The hype is louder. And somewhere between the two, most practitioners have been left holding subscriptions they do not fully use, systems that worked in the demo but stumbled on the first real client file, and a vague sense that they are either behind the curve or being sold to — and they are not sure which.

Here is how I know the playing field is more open than anyone is admitting publicly: as I was finishing this book in March 2026, KPMG — one of the largest professional services firms in the world — announced what they called AI Spark Innovation awards: cash prizes for employees who could demonstrate an incredible thing they had done with AI. Business Insider reported that the awards were designed, in the words of KPMG's own U.S. vice chair of advisory, to unlock grassroots innovation. Not a research lab. Not a dedicated innovation team. Cash prizes for grassroots innovation — because even at their scale, the workflows do not exist yet. If the Big Four are still searching for their own AI workflows, the window for every other firm is wider than the conference keynotes suggest. The firm that builds deliberately in the next twenty-four months — regardless of size — is the firm that wins.

I wrote this book because I could not find the one I needed.

Not a book about what AI is. Not a breathless manifesto about how the profession is about to be disrupted. Not a vendor whitepaper dressed up as strategy. I needed a book written by someone who had actually sat at the desk — prepared the returns, managed the client calls, reviewed the workpapers — and then built the AI systems on top of that practice. Someone who understood both sides of the equation not because they had studied them, but because they had lived them.

I have a Big 4 background, an active CPA practice, and I build AI workflow systems for accounting firms through Milairo — including the systems I use on my own clients. That is not a credential list. It is the reason this book is different from the ones already on the shelf.

That equation is the spine of this book. Every chapter is an answer to one question: what does it take to get your practice to the point where that equation describes how your work actually moves?

> *AI handles production → You apply judgment → Judgment = the liability → Liability = the signature → Signature = the value.*

Who This Book Is For

This book is written for the practitioner making AI decisions for their firm. Whether you are a managing partner at an independent practice, a workflow manager at a regional firm, or a senior professional at a large firm trying to build something that does not exist yet inside your organization — if you are the person who has to figure out what AI actually means for how your team works, this book is for you.

You are not a technologist. You are not an AI researcher. You are a practitioner — licensed, credentialed, accountable — who is trying to make good decisions about AI in your practice next quarter, not next decade.

You have probably seen the demos. You may have bought the subscriptions. Something probably worked, partially, for a while. And you are now somewhere between cautiously optimistic and quietly skeptical, looking for someone to tell you — plainly, without selling you anything — what is actually real and what to do about it.

That is exactly who I wrote this for.

This book is not for data engineers, AI researchers, or consultants who want a theoretical framework. It is for the practitioner who signs the returns, manages the staff, and has to make the AI decision themselves — without a CTO, without a dedicated IT budget, and without time to waste on systems that do not survive contact with a real client file.

The Framework at the Center of This Book

Everything in this book is organized around a single framework: the three tiers of accounting AI.

TIER 1 — AUTOMATION

It is the removal of repetitive manual tasks — the chatbot layer inside your practice management software, the AI categorization feature AppFolio or QuickBooks quietly shipped last year, the Copilot button that appeared in your Excel ribbon, the intelligent suggestions Intuit added to the transaction feed. Every major platform has bolted some version of this on. It is a commodity. It is table stakes. And it is almost exclusively what is being sold to accounting firms right now, often dressed up as something far more sophisticated.

TIER 2 — INTELLIGENCE

It is domain knowledge encoded as software — tax law classification, multi-entity workflow logic, workpaper standards, professional judgment applied at scale. Very few systems are genuinely here. The firms that build toward Tier 2 in the next two years will have a competitive advantage that is extremely difficult to replicate.

TIER 3 — JUDGMENT

It is proactive advisory — surfacing the question before the client thinks to ask it, identifying the pattern before it becomes a problem, making the strategic recommendation that only years of return preparation makes possible. This is where the profession is going. Almost no one is here yet.

The core insight this book is built around is simple: most systems being sold to accounting firms are Tier 1 dressed up as Tier 2. The marketing language sounds like intelligence. The underlying system is automation. This book teaches you to tell the difference — and gives you a clear path for building toward Tier 2 and Tier 3 in your own firm.

How This Book Is Organized

PART ONE — THE MENTAL MODEL

Explains what AI actually is and is not in the context of an accounting practice, why most demos fail on real client files, and how the three-tier framework works in practice. Read this first, even if you feel like you already know what AI is. You may find you know less than you thought, or more than the vendors have given you credit for.

PART TWO — THE FIRM AUDIT

Walks through your practice workflow by workflow: intake, bookkeeping, classification, workpaper prep, review. It gives you a diagnostic for where your firm actually sits on the tier map and a prioritized list of what to address first. You will leave this section with a concrete plan, not a vague aspiration.

PART THREE — THE IMPLEMENTATION PLAYBOOK

Covers the practical reality of executing: how to evaluate systems without getting sold, how to run a pilot without disrupting your practice, how to bring staff along, and how to price the efficiency gains in a way that actually improves your firm's economics. The final chapter describes what the firm looks like in three years if you execute this well — and what it looks like if you wait.

The appendix contains three tools you can use immediately: a vendor evaluation scorecard, a workflow mapping template, and a ninety-day pilot checklist. These are not theoretical frameworks. I use versions of all three in my own practice and in engagements with client firms.

The Framework in Use

Every chapter in this book uses the three-tier framework as a reference point. When we walk through your firm's workflows in Part Two, we will map each workflow to a tier and identify the specific points where Tier 1 automation is appropriate and where Tier 2 intelligence is required. When we cover tool evaluation in Part Three, the tier framework is the primary diagnostic.

The framework is also the vocabulary you need to have a different kind of conversation with vendors. When you can ask a vendor which tier their tool operates at — and follow up with the specific questions that test the answer — you change the dynamic of the evaluation. You are no longer being sold to. You are running a diagnostic. That shift in position is one of the most practical things this book can give you.

Before you go further, a check: can you already place the AI tools your firm is currently using on the tier map? Run through them. The AI feature in your practice management software — Tier 1. The document capture layer — Tier 1. The categorization engine inside the property management platform — Tier 1. If you have anything that flags uncertainty, draws an explicit judgment line, and routes decisions to you with specific reasoning — that is moving toward Tier 2. If you do not have anything in that category yet, Part Two will show you exactly where to start.

One Last Thing Before We Start

AI will not replace the accountant. I want to say that clearly, not as reassurance, but as a structural observation. The licensed professional who signs the work, accepts the liability, and exercises judgment in the face of ambiguity is not being automated. The profession is not going away.

What is changing — and changing fast — is what the practice looks like inside. The firms that understand this and build deliberately will find that AI makes them better at the parts of this work that actually require a credentialed professional, by eliminating the parts that do not. The firms that wait, or that buy systems without a framework for evaluating them, will find themselves doing the same work for lower margins as the market adjusts around them.

That is the real stakes of this conversation. Not disruption. Not replacement. Differentiation.

Economists call this the Jevons Paradox. In 1865, William Stanley Jevons observed that making steam engines more efficient did not reduce coal consumption — it expanded it, because cheaper energy unlocked entirely new uses that had previously been uneconomical. The same dynamic is arriving at the accounting profession. As the cost of producing clean financial data collapses, the demand for what sits above that data — judgment, analysis, planning, advisory —

expands rather than contracts. The practitioners who understand this are not asking whether AI will take their work. They are asking what work becomes possible when the production layer costs nothing.

That is the question this book is built to answer.

Victor A. De la Cruz, CPA
Founder, Milairo
milairo.com

CHAPTER 1

The Demo Problem

Every CPA who has bought an AI tool in the last three years has a version of the same story. The demo was clean. The interface was fast. The vendor showed a CSV going in and a categorized ledger coming out in seconds. The sales rep used the phrase 'game-changer' at least once. You signed up. You ran your first real client file through it. Something went wrong — not catastrophically, not obviously, but enough that you had to go back and check everything anyway.

That experience has a name. This chapter is about why it keeps happening, what it reveals about how AI tools are built and sold, and how to use that understanding to evaluate every tool you will look at from here forward.

CHAPTER 1 · THE DEMO PROBLEM

Demo		Reality		Result
Clean Data	→	**Real Files**	→	**Gap Exposed**
CONTROLLED		MESSY		BREAKS HERE

The demo works because the data is perfect. Your clients' data never is.

Why Every Demo Works

AI demos are not dishonest. That is what makes them dangerous. The tool genuinely does what the vendor shows you. The problem is what they choose to show you.

Demo data is clean data. It is a single entity. One bank account. Transactions that match categories in an obvious way. No reconciliation gaps. No co-mingled operating and personal expenses. No multi-jurisdictional entities with an AppFolio export sitting next to a QuickBooks file that has not been reconciled in eight months. The demo shows you the tool running on data that was built to make the tool look good. Your client data was built by your clients — which means it looks nothing like that.

The vendors know this. They are not hiding it. They are showing you the best case, which is their job. Your job is to understand what the tool actually does when the data looks like your clients' data — and to know what questions to ask before you commit.

> *Demo data is clean data. Client data is not. That gap is where most AI tools break — and where most purchasing decisions go wrong.*

The Confidence Problem

There is a specific failure mode in AI tools that is worse than getting things wrong loudly. It is getting things wrong quietly. A system that crashes or produces obvious errors is easy to catch. A system that runs confidently and produces plausible-but-incorrect output is a professional liability.

Most accounting AI features being sold today — the categorization layer inside AppFolio, the Intuit Assist chatbot inside QuickBooks, the Copilot button that appeared in your Excel ribbon, the AI module your practice management platform added in the last release — are built on general-purpose models that have been fine-tuned for common financial transactions. They are reasonably good at the obvious stuff. They are significantly less reliable on the decisions that actually require a CPA — the repair versus capital improvement call on a rental property, the passive loss exposure question on a multi-entity portfolio, the classification judgment when the same bank account funds three properties across two states.

These are not edge cases in a CPA practice. These are Tuesday.

The tool does not know it is uncertain. It classifies confidently regardless of whether it is right. And if you do not know where it is likely to be wrong — which requires knowing the underlying tax logic well enough to spot the error — you will miss it. This is not an argument against using AI. It is an argument for understanding what kind of AI you are using and what it was actually trained to do.

What AI Adoption Actually Looks Like Right Now

AI adoption in accounting firms jumped from nine percent in 2024 to forty-one percent in 2025. That number gets cited at every conference as evidence that the profession has crossed a threshold. What it does not tell you is what 'adoption' means. In most surveys, adoption means a firm has purchased a tool with AI features. It does not mean the tool is used consistently. It does not mean it has changed how the firm operates. It does not mean anyone has measured whether it saves time.

Karbon's 2026 State of AI in Accounting report found that firms using AI save an average of eighty-two minutes per person per day. That is a real number and it is significant — over a tax season, across a five-person team, that is weeks of recovered capacity. But that number comes from firms that have implemented AI thoughtfully, in the right workflows, with appropriate review processes. It does not come from firms that bought a tool, ran it on a few client files, decided it was not quite right, and let the subscription renew quietly in the background.

The gap between 'firm that purchased AI' and 'firm that implemented AI well' is the gap this book is about.

> *Forty-one percent of firms have purchased AI. A fraction of that number have implemented it in a way that changed how they work. The gap between those two numbers is the opportunity.*

The Vendor's Incentive Problem

Software vendors are not in the business of telling you where their tools fail. This is not a cynical observation — it is a structural reality. Their job is to show you the upside. Your job is to find the downside before you commit.

The accounting software market has a specific version of this problem. AppFolio added AI categorization. QuickBooks shipped Intuit Assist. Karbon launched an AI bookkeeper. Canopy released a bookkeeping module. Ramp, Bill, and Emburse all made AI announcements in rapid succession. Microsoft put Copilot inside Excel, Word, and Teams. Every platform your firm already uses has added an AI feature. The race to ship has outpaced the underlying capability to deliver — and the firms buying these features are often the last to find out.

When every vendor says their product uses AI, the word stops being useful. What matters is not whether a tool uses AI — everything uses AI now — but what kind of AI, trained on what data, validated against what standards, and reviewed by whom before the output touches a client file. Those are the questions the demo will not answer. The next chapter gives you the framework to ask them.

The Real Question Behind Every Demo

When you sit down for an AI tool demo, you will be shown speed, accuracy, and ease. Those are the right things to show. They are also the things that are easiest to optimize for in a controlled demonstration.

The questions that actually determine whether a tool will work in your practice are different. They are not about the tool's best-case performance. They are about its failure modes. What does it do when the data is incomplete? When two entities are co-mingled in the same account? When a transaction could reasonably be classified two different ways depending on facts the system does not have access to? When the client has not reconciled in eight months?

Ask a vendor those questions and watch what happens. A tool with real depth will have real answers — specific failure states, specific confidence thresholds, specific review triggers. A Tier 1 tool dressed as Tier 2 will give you a general answer about human oversight and the importance of review. Both answers are technically correct. Only one of them tells you something useful.

This is the demo problem. Not that the demos are dishonest — they are not. But that the questions being answered in the demo are not the same questions you need answered before you deploy a tool on client files you are professionally responsible for.

What This Means for How You Evaluate Tools

The practical implication of everything in this chapter is simple: do not evaluate AI tools in demo conditions. Evaluate them on your data.

Take a real client file — one that is representative of the complexity you actually deal with, not your cleanest client. Run it through the tool before you commit to a subscription. Document what it gets right, what it gets wrong, and how confident it was about the things it got wrong. That last part is the most important. A tool that knows it is uncertain — that flags low-confidence classifications for review rather than committing to them — is a fundamentally different kind of tool than one that is wrong with equal confidence on everything.

Part Three of this book covers the full pilot methodology. But the principle starts here: the demo is not the test. The test is the test.

Where This Leaves Us

The demo problem is not going away. As AI tools get better, the demos will get more impressive. The gap between demo performance and production performance will narrow over time — but it will not close entirely, because demo data will always be cleaner than client data, and vendor incentives will always favor showing you the upside.

What changes is your ability to navigate that gap. The three-tier framework in the next chapter is the tool for doing that. Once you understand the difference between automation, intelligence, and judgment — and once you can identify which tier a tool actually operates at, as opposed to which tier its marketing claims — the demo stops being a sales event and starts being a diagnostic. You know what to look for. You know what questions to ask. You know what the right answer sounds like.

That is the shift this book is designed to create. Not skepticism about AI — the tools are real and the opportunity is real. But informed evaluation instead of impressed evaluation. The difference between those two things, over the next two years, is the difference between a firm that builds a durable advantage and a firm that collects subscriptions.

CHAPTER 2

The Three Tiers

The most expensive mistake a firm can make with AI is buying the wrong tier. Not the wrong vendor — the wrong tier. A Tier 1 tool in a workflow that needs Tier 2 does not just underperform. It creates work. It produces confident output that requires professional review on every line, which means you have added a step to the process rather than removed one. You are paying for a tool that makes your job harder.

This chapter defines the three tiers precisely — not as marketing categories, but as a diagnostic tool. By the end of it you will be able to look at any AI product, sit through any demo, and place it accurately on the tier map. That skill is worth more than any individual tool decision you will make in the next two years.

The data suggests the profession needs this diagnostic badly. According to reporting published by the Pennsylvania Institute of CPAs, businesses are routing 77 percent of their AI activity into task automation — not collaboration, not strategic problem-solving, not advisory support. Task automation. The profession is not failing to adopt AI. It is failing to understand which tier of AI it is adopting. The result is a widespread investment in Tier 1 capability that gets measured against Tier 2 expectations — and almost always disappoints.

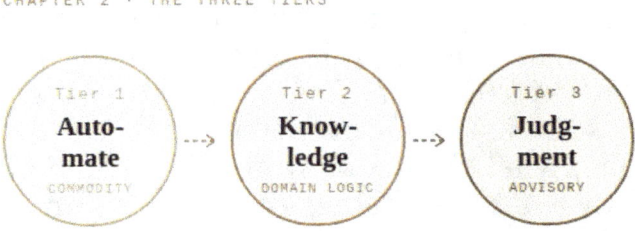

Each tier requires the one before it. Most firms stop at Tier 1.

TIER 1 — AUTOMATION

Tier 1 is the removal of repetitive manual tasks through pattern recognition. It does not require understanding. It requires pattern matching — and modern AI is extraordinarily good at pattern matching on structured data.

The simplest way to define Tier 1: it knows categories. It looks at a transaction and asks — what does this look like? A $4,200 Home Depot charge looks like repairs. Categorized. Confident. Done. What Tier 1 looks like in practice: the AI categorization layer inside QuickBooks or AppFolio, the document capture system that pulls data from a PDF and populates fields, the bank feed reconciliation that matches deposits to invoices, the Copilot button in Excel that summarizes a spreadsheet you already built. These are all Tier 1. They are useful. They save time on routine tasks. And they are almost universally what is being marketed as AI transformation.

The defining characteristic of Tier 1 is this: it does not know what it does not know. That same $4,200 Home Depot charge — Tier 1 does not ask what property, what work was done, what the client's capitalization policy is, or what the business context requires. It matches the pattern and moves on. Confidently. It does not know whether the payment represents a repair or a capital improvement. It does not know the facts and circumstances that determine the correct treatment under the applicable standard. It does not know that getting this wrong has consequences — for the financials, for the tax return, for the audit file, for the client. Tier 1 knows categories. It does not know consequences.

> *Tier 1 does not know what it does not know. That is not a flaw in the tool — it is the definition of the tier. The flaw is buying Tier 1 for a job that requires Tier 2.*

Tier 1 tools are not bad tools. They are the right tools for the right workflows — high-volume, low-judgment tasks where the cost of a wrong classification is low and the review process catches errors before they matter. The problem is not Tier 1 itself. The problem is that Tier 1 is routinely sold as Tier 2, deployed in workflows that require judgment, and blamed for failures that were predictable from the beginning.

There is a structural reason Tier 1 fails in judgment-intensive workflows, and it was stated precisely by a group of CPA academics writing in the Pennsylvania CPA Journal: unlike a practitioner, AI does not say "it depends." It tends to be definitive in its pronouncements. That is the technical signature of a Tier 1 system — confident output regardless of the underlying complexity of the question. In accounting, where the answer almost always depends on facts and circumstances, a tool that cannot express uncertainty is a tool that cannot be trusted with consequential decisions.

TIER 2 — INTELLIGENCE

Tier 2 is domain knowledge encoded as software. Where Tier 1 knows categories, Tier 2 knows consequences. It does not look at a transaction and ask what does this look like — it asks what does this mean, and what does a practitioner need to know about it. It is rules, logic, and professional judgment built by practitioners who understand the underlying requirements, applied consistently at scale.

The difference between Tier 1 and Tier 2 is best understood through the same $4,200 Home Depot charge. Tier 1 categorizes it as repairs and moves on. Tier 2 asks: what property is this for? What was the work? Is this a repair or a capital improvement — and does the answer change depending on the client's capitalization policy, the asset's existing basis, or the applicable reporting standard? Those are not categorization questions. They are judgment questions. Without those answers, the right output is not a confident classification — it is a flag for practitioner review with the specific questions that need answering, and a clear note on what is at stake if the wrong answer is chosen.

That distinction — categories versus consequences — is the operational definition of Tier 2. A Tier 2 system knows the boundary of its own competence. It automates what can be automated, flags what requires judgment, and tells you specifically why it is flagging and what is at stake if the judgment goes the wrong way. It replaces not the data entry clerk but the first hour of the practitioner's review — the part where they ask: what do I need to look at here, and why.

Other examples of genuine Tier 2 capability across practice contexts: an audit tool that flags a variance and explains whether the most likely cause is a timing difference, a posting error, or a pattern that warrants further testing — rather than simply surfacing the number. A classification engine that distinguishes between entities in a co-mingled account based on ownership structure rather than transaction description alone. A system that tracks whether expenses meet a client's own capitalization policy and alerts the reviewer when a judgment call is required — before the workpaper is finalized. On the tax side: a system that identifies that the same $4,200 Home Depot charge requires 263(a) analysis given the client's capitalization policy and asset basis — rather than defaulting to a confident expense classification and moving on. These capabilities require professional knowledge baked into the system architecture — not just a language model running on top of a general-purpose dataset.

> *Very few tools are genuinely at Tier 2. The firms that build toward Tier 2 in the next two years will have a competitive advantage that is extremely difficult to replicate — because domain knowledge compounds, and generic tools cannot catch up without it.*

This distinction is not unique to accounting. A senior finance executive posted to LinkedIn recently that her firm's AI deployment had settled into a clear division: the agents handled the pull, humans handled the judgment. The post drew significant engagement — not because the observation was surprising, but because it named something practitioners across industries were experiencing and had not yet said plainly. The tier boundary is real. Every professional who works alongside AI encounters it. The accounting profession's specific challenge is that its tier boundary carries professional liability, not just operational risk. Judgment calls in accounting have legal and ethical consequences. That is what makes a clean tier architecture — one that knows what it knows and flags what it does not — more than a design preference. It is a professional requirement.

Tier 2 is where competitive advantage lives. It is also where almost nobody is right now. The tools that are genuinely at Tier 2 are narrow — built for specific workflows, specific client types, specific areas of the tax code — because that is what real domain knowledge requires. A system that claims to be Tier 2 across every workflow is almost certainly Tier 1 in a better suit.

TIER 3 — JUDGMENT

Tier 3 is proactive advisory. It is the system that surfaces the question before the client thinks to ask it. The pattern it identifies before it becomes a problem. The strategic observation that only becomes possible after years of seeing the same client's data in context — and that, increasingly, AI can surface faster than any human reviewing a file in isolation.

A Tier 3 example: a system that reviews three years of a client's financial data, identifies a pattern of increasing owner compensation against declining retained earnings in a services business, and surfaces a question — has the client's compensation structure been reviewed against reasonable compensation benchmarks given the entity type and current margins? That is not automation. It is not even intelligence in the narrow sense. It is judgment — the synthesis of historical data, tax law knowledge, and forward-looking pattern recognition that a good practitioner provides in an advisory relationship.

Almost no commercial tool is at Tier 3 today. The technology is beginning to make it possible — large language models with access to structured client data and deep tax logic can start to approximate this kind of synthesis. But the infrastructure required — clean data, deep domain logic, year-over-year context — does not exist in most firms yet. You cannot reach Tier 3 without first building Tier 2. And you cannot build Tier 2 without first understanding where your Tier 1 tools end.

This is where the profession is going. The practitioner who can combine their own judgment with a Tier 3 system — who can ask the right question of the right data and synthesize the answer into an advisory conversation — is not being replaced by AI. They are being amplified by it. That is the version of this profession that survives and thrives. But getting there requires building the foundation correctly.

A Note on Agents and Chatbots

The two words you will hear most in AI accounting demos right now are agents and chat. A platform announces it has AI agents. Another adds a chatbot so you can ask questions about your books. Both sound like Tier 2 or Tier 3. Neither word tells you which tier you are actually looking at.

An agent, in the way most accounting platforms use the term, is a system that executes a sequence of tasks automatically — pull the bank feed, match to invoices, post to the general ledger, flag exceptions. That is workflow automation. It is useful. It is Tier 1. The agent is doing a chain of Tier 1 tasks without waiting for you to click between them. The autonomy is real. The intelligence is not.

A chatbot that answers questions about your books is drawing from whatever data the underlying system has. If the underlying system is a general ledger with no tax domain knowledge, the chatbot's answers reflect that. Ask it whether a $4,200 contractor payment should be expensed or capitalized and it will give you a plausible-sounding answer based on pattern matching — not IRC 263(a) analysis. The interface is conversational. The intelligence is still Tier 1.

> *The interface is not the intelligence. An agent that executes Tier 1 tasks is still Tier 1. A chatbot drawing from Tier 1 data is still Tier 1. Ask what the system knows — not how it talks.*

This matters because agents and chatbots are the current vocabulary of Tier 1 tools trying to sound like Tier 2. When you hear those words in a demo, they are not evidence of tier — they are a prompt to ask deeper questions. What does the agent actually know? What is the chatbot drawing from? Does either of them understand the consequences of the decisions they are making — or just the categories?

How to Tell the Difference in Practice

The tier a tool claims to be and the tier it actually operates at are frequently not the same. Every vendor wants to be Tier 2. Most tools are Tier 1. Here is how to tell the difference in a real evaluation.

Ask about uncertainty. A Tier 1 tool classifies everything with uniform confidence. A Tier 2 tool has a confidence model — it knows when it is less certain and it behaves differently in those cases. Ask the vendor: what does the system do when it encounters a transaction it cannot classify confidently? If the answer is that it assigns the most likely category and moves on, you are looking at Tier 1. If the answer is that it flags the transaction with a specific reason and routes it for review, you may be looking at Tier 2.

Ask about the judgment line. Every firm workflow has a point where automation ends and professional judgment begins. Ask the vendor where their tool draws that line — and whether the line is explicit in the system architecture or left to the user to manage. A Tier 2 system has a designed judgment boundary. A Tier 1 system pretends the boundary does not exist.

Ask about domain specificity. Tier 2 intelligence is narrow by definition. A system with genuine tax logic for one practice area does not also have genuine tax logic for manufacturing cost accounting, nonprofit fund accounting, and international transfer pricing. If a vendor claims their system handles every practice area with equal intelligence, probe the depth. Ask for a specific example — not a use case from their marketing materials, but a specific transaction type in your actual workflows — and ask exactly what the system does with it.

Ask who built the domain knowledge. Tier 2 tools are built by people who understand both the technology and the underlying professional standards. Ask the vendor who designed the tax logic in their system. Ask whether practitioners were involved in building it or only in testing it. The answer tells you a great deal about whether you are looking at genuine domain intelligence or a general-purpose model with accounting-flavored marketing.

Where Most Firms Are Right Now

Most firms that have adopted AI are operating at Tier 1. They have connected a bank feed to a categorization engine. They have added a document capture layer to their intake process. They have turned on the AI features inside the software they were already using. This is not nothing — Tier 1 automation recovers real time on real tasks. But it is not the competitive advantage the conference keynotes promised.

The firms that are beginning to move toward Tier 2 are building custom workflows — not buying off-the-shelf tools and hoping they fit, but designing systems around the specific judgment requirements of their firm. They are thinking about the judgment line explicitly. They are building review processes that assume AI will be wrong on specific categories of decisions and designing the workflow accordingly. These firms are not more sophisticated technologically. They are more disciplined about understanding what the tool can and cannot do.

The gap between Tier 1 and Tier 2 is not a technology gap. It is a knowledge gap. The firms that close it first will not necessarily be the ones with the largest technology budgets. They will be the ones that understand their own workflows well enough to know where the judgment line is — and that understand the tools well enough to know which side of the line each one belongs on.

Most firms that have adopted AI today are running a hybrid model whether they know it or not. Tier 1 handles the pull — categorization, data capture, bank feed matching. Tier 2 is handled by humans — the practitioner who reviews the output, applies professional judgment, and decides what the numbers actually mean. This arrangement works. It is also expensive, because it leaves the most time-intensive part of the workflow — the judgment layer — entirely in human hands.

The next move is not to remove the human from that review. It is to encode Tier 2 into the AI layer so the human review is elevated rather than eliminated. Instead of a practitioner asking — what do I need to look at here, and why? — the system asks it first. It surfaces the consequences, not just the categories. The practitioner still approves. Still signs. Still decides. But they are reviewing a system that has already applied the relevant domain logic and flagged what matters — rather than starting from a confident output that may or may not be correct.

> *The goal is not to replace the practitioner's judgment. It is to build a system that knows enough to ask the right questions before the practitioner ever opens the file.*

This is a design choice, not a technology constraint. The components exist: accounting-specific logic, connections to practice management and bookkeeping platforms, structured client data, and the domain knowledge of practitioners who have spent years in specific practice areas. What has been missing is the deliberate architecture — someone who understands the tax code deeply enough to know which decisions require Tier 2 logic, and who understands the technology well enough to build it. That is the gap the next generation of practice-built software is beginning to close.

The Framework in Use

Every chapter in this book uses the three-tier framework as a reference point. When we walk through your firm's workflows in Part Two, we will map each workflow to a tier and identify the specific points where Tier 1 automation is appropriate and where Tier 2 intelligence is required. When we cover tool evaluation in Part Three, the tier framework is the primary diagnostic.

The framework is also the vocabulary you need to have a different kind of conversation with vendors. When you can ask a vendor which tier their tool operates at — and follow up with the specific questions that test the answer — you change the dynamic of the evaluation. You are no longer being sold to. You are running a diagnostic. That shift in position is one of the most practical things this book can give you.

That shift in position depends on one more thing — understanding why accounting AI operates under constraints that general-purpose AI cannot meet, and why getting that wrong carries consequences that go beyond a bad demo.

CHAPTER 3

Why Accounting AI Is Different

Every profession that uses AI faces the question of what happens when the AI is wrong. In most contexts, the answer is straightforward: you fix it and move on. A marketing recommendation that misses the mark costs a campaign. A logistics optimization that underperforms costs some efficiency. The error is recoverable, the cost is bounded, and the professional involved is not personally liable for the machine's output.

Accounting does not work that way. When AI produces a wrong answer in an accounting context — a misclassified asset, an overlooked passive loss, a capitalization decision made without the relevant facts — the consequences run downstream. Into the financial statements. Into the tax return. Into the client's business decisions made from that data. Into a potential audit, a regulatory examination, or a malpractice claim. And at the end of that chain stands a licensed professional whose name is on the engagement letter.

That is the structural difference. Not that accounting is more complex than medicine, law, or engineering — each of those professions carries its own version of this weight. It is that accounting's liability structure is unusually direct. The practitioner is not just advising. They are certifying. The signature on a tax return or a set of financial statements is a professional assertion of accuracy and completeness. AI does not change that assertion. It just changes how the work behind it gets done — and whether the practitioner fully understands what the AI contributed to it.

> *The AI does not hold a license. The AI does not sign the return. The AI does not appear before the IRS. The practitioner does. That asymmetry is the entire reason the judgment line matters.*

The AICPA member insurance program has stated it plainly: indiscriminate reliance on AI output when delivering services — without critically analyzing whether the result is correct — may lead to errors, omissions, and potential professional liability claims. That is not a theoretical risk. It is the operational description of what happens when a Tier 1 tool is deployed in a Tier 2 workflow without a designed judgment boundary. Understanding why that boundary exists — and what it takes to build it correctly — is what this chapter is about.

The Liability Layer

The profession has not been slow to recognize the liability exposure. It has been slow to connect it to the specific design decisions that create or eliminate the risk. Most AI governance conversations in accounting firms focus on data privacy — whether client information is being sent to a third-party server, whether the vendor's terms of service are acceptable, whether the tool is SOC 2 compliant. Those are real questions and worth asking. But they are not the liability question that matters most.

The liability question that matters most is simpler: does the system know when it does not know? A Tier 1 system categorizes transactions and produces output. It does not flag the transaction that could reasonably be classified two ways depending on facts the system was not given. It does not pause when a payment could be an expense or a capital asset depending on context it was never asked to consider. It does not recognize that the same transaction treated one way on the financial statements may need to be treated differently on the tax return — or that getting that difference wrong is not a rounding error. It processes what it has and moves on — confidently, completely, and without visible uncertainty.

That confidence is the liability exposure. Not the wrong answer itself — practitioners catch wrong answers in review. The exposure is the wrong answer that looks right. The output that is formatted correctly, internally consistent, and professionally presented — but built on an incomplete set of facts that the system never knew to ask for. A practitioner reviewing that output without understanding the system's limitations is not reviewing. They are approving. And approval is a professional act with professional consequences.

A venture capitalist focused on CFO technology captured the three-level structure of this problem in a single public observation about what the largest financial institutions are building with AI: parsing data, applying rules, exercising judgment. Three lines. Three levels. The investment community has arrived at the same architecture independently — because that is the shape of the work, and the liability exposure lives precisely at the boundary between the second level and the third.

The Confidence Problem in a Profession Built on "It Depends"

There is a specific mismatch between how AI systems produce output and how accounting work actually gets done. AI systems — particularly the general-purpose large language models that most firms are experimenting with — are trained to produce confident, complete-sounding answers. They do not naturally express uncertainty. They do not say "it depends" the way a practitioner would. They fill the space with something that sounds authoritative whether or not the underlying answer is correct.

Accounting is a profession built on "it depends." The answer to almost every consequential question — how to classify this transaction, whether this expense is deductible, how to treat this lease, what this variance means — depends on facts and circumstances that a general-purpose AI cannot be assumed to know or to ask for. A system that produces a confident answer without first establishing those facts is not a Tier 2 system. It is a Tier 1 system with good presentation. And in accounting, the presentation is the most dangerous part — because it looks right to anyone who does not already know the answer.

A group of CPA academics writing in a peer-reviewed journal made the same observation from direct experience: unlike a practitioner, AI tends to be definitive in its pronouncements. For accountants with less experience in the area they are researching, those responses are particularly challenging because they can be a compelling read. The issue is not that the AI is always wrong. It is that the AI does not signal when it is wrong — and in accounting, that silence is professionally dangerous.

> *A Tier 2 system does not just produce answers. It produces answers with a confidence model attached — one that knows when to flag, when to ask, and when to route the decision to a human who can apply judgment to facts the system cannot fully evaluate.*

This is the technical requirement that separates accounting AI from general-purpose AI. It is not about raw capability — modern language models can process accounting concepts with remarkable fluency. It is about the architecture of uncertainty. A system built for accounting needs to know what it does not know, express that uncertainty in terms a practitioner can act on, and draw the judgment line at the right place. General-purpose tools do not do this by default. Building it in requires deliberate design by someone who understands both the technology and the professional standards.

MCP removed the infrastructure barrier. Domain knowledge is now the moat.

The Infrastructure Shift That Changed the Calculation

For most of the past decade, the barrier to building Tier 2 accounting AI was not knowledge — it was infrastructure. Connecting an AI system to the actual data sources a practitioner works with required custom integrations for every platform: one for the general ledger, one for the document management system, one for the practice management software, one for the client portal. Each integration was an engineering project. The total cost made Tier 2 tools viable only for large enterprises or well-funded startups. Most practitioners were locked out.

That changed in November 2024 when Anthropic introduced the Model Context Protocol — MCP. The concept is straightforward: a standardized way for AI systems to discover and interact with external software, data sources, and tools without requiring custom integrations for each one. Think of it as a universal connector — instead of building a separate bridge between your AI system and every platform it needs to access, MCP provides a common language that any compliant system can speak.

The accounting profession took notice when Google, OpenAI, and Microsoft all announced native MCP support in rapid succession. MCP servers appeared for QuickBooks, Xero, SAP, and dozens of other platforms that practitioners already use. A CPA writing in the Pennsylvania CPA Journal described the shift precisely: MCP is a universal translator between AI's natural language understanding and the functional reality of your business systems. Xero's MCP implementation alone exposes more than 40 functions — from retrieving a chart of accounts to updating a payroll timesheet line — all accessible to an AI agent without a single custom integration.

For practitioners building Tier 2 tools, the implication is significant. The infrastructure work that once required significant engineering investment now takes a fraction of the time. The connection layer between an AI intelligence system and a firm's actual practice data — the bank feed, the general ledger, the client documents, the workpaper system — is no longer a barrier. It is a configuration. That shift collapsed the cost of entry for practice-built software in a way that has not yet fully registered in the profession's understanding of what is possible.

> *MCP did not make Tier 2 accounting AI easier to imagine. It made it faster to build. The window between "this is theoretically possible" and "this exists and works" collapsed from years to months.*

The governance implications run alongside the opportunity. A technology and practice management publication noted in early 2026 that MCP also introduces new risks: over-permissioned access tokens that give AI agents too much authority over connected systems, missing audit trails when agent actions are not logged, and the absence of enforced human review for high-stakes decisions unless specifically configured. These are not reasons to avoid MCP — they are reasons to approach it with the same professional rigor you would bring to any system that touches client data. The practitioners who understand both the capability and the governance requirements will be the ones who build and evaluate tools others can trust.

The Data Is the Moat

Geoffrey Doempke is a CPA and CFO who spent years building the data infrastructure for his finance function himself — writing SQL, building pipelines, creating the architecture that made his organization's numbers reliable. He was, by his own description, irreplaceable. Then he automated that work. Not because the work was unimportant — it was essential — but because once the infrastructure was clean, the AI could do it. And once the AI was doing it, he could stop being the gatekeeper and start doing the work a CFO is actually supposed to do.

His observation about what made that transition possible — shared in a LinkedIn post that drew significant engagement from finance and accounting professionals — is the most important practical insight in this chapter: the data is the moat. AI is only as good as what you feed it. Point it at messy data and you get garbage faster. But build clean infrastructure and AI turns your entire team into analysts overnight.

This is the part of the AI conversation that most vendors skip, because it is not their problem to solve. A vendor sells you a system. What that system runs on is your data — your chart of accounts, your client files, your transaction history, your workpaper structure. If that foundation is inconsistent, incomplete, or poorly organized, the AI will process it confidently and produce output that reflects the mess. The tool does not know the data is bad. It just knows what it sees.

For accounting firms, this means the work that precedes AI deployment is often more consequential than the deployment itself. Standardizing your chart of accounts. Cleaning up client data that has accumulated inconsistencies over years. Building workpaper templates that produce structured, machine-readable output rather than freeform documents. Establishing naming conventions and filing structures that an AI system can navigate reliably. None of this is glamorous. None of it shows up in a vendor demo. All of it determines whether the AI you eventually deploy produces trusted output or confident noise.

> *The firms that will lead in AI are not necessarily the ones that move first. They are the ones that build the foundation correctly before they move.*

Doempke's other observation from that same post is equally important: the Tableau guy is dead. The SQL gatekeeper is dead. The professional whose value came from being the intermediary between data and decision — the person who could run the query, build the report, pull the number — is being automated out of that role. Not because they are less skilled, but because the skill is no longer scarce. When the AI can answer "what is our LTV to CAC by cohort" before the coffee finishes brewing, the value has shifted from pulling the data to knowing what to do with it.

For accounting practitioners, the parallel is direct. The value that comes from being the person who can navigate a complex tax return or reconcile a difficult set of books — the Tier 1 and low-Tier 2 work — is becoming commoditized by the same infrastructure shift. What remains scarce, and what AI cannot replicate, is the judgment that sits above it: the practitioner who knows what question to ask of the data, what the answer means in context, and what the client needs to do about it.

Governance Is the New Adoption

For a period, the competitive question in accounting AI was whether you had adopted it. Firms that had connected AI systems to their workflows were ahead. Firms that had not were behind. That framing made adoption the goal — get the tools in place, get the staff using them, get the workflows running. The assumption was that adoption was the hard part.

A consultant writing for the Pennsylvania Institute of CPAs captured the shift precisely: competitive advantages will shift from adoption to governance, training, and thoughtful oversight of AI-enabled processes. Firms that invest early in controls and education will reduce risk while increasing efficiency. The race to adopt is over. The race to govern has begun.

Governance in this context means something specific. It is not a compliance exercise or a policy document nobody reads. It is the set of designed decisions about where AI operates in your workflow, where the judgment line sits, what the human review process looks like, and how you know when the AI has reached the boundary of its competence. It is the difference between a firm that has AI running in its processes and a firm that knows what its AI is doing.

A legal technology leader working in a regulated financial institution wrote publicly about what governance looks like in practice: every organization has someone pasting confidential information into a free AI tool right now. The question is not whether AI is being used — it is whether it is being used with appropriate controls. For accounting firms, the stakes are higher than most: client data includes tax returns, financial statements, Social Security numbers, business plans, and estate documents. The professional obligations around that data — under Circular 230, state privacy laws, and the AICPA's own standards — do not pause because a staff member used a convenient tool.

The governance argument is not a reason to slow down. It is a reason to build deliberately. A firm that deploys AI with clear data handling policies, explicit judgment boundaries, and documented review processes is not moving slower than a firm that deploys without those things. It is building something that will hold under scrutiny — from clients, from regulators, and from the professional standards that have always governed this work.

The Window Is Open

The infrastructure barrier that once made Tier 2 accounting AI the exclusive domain of enterprise technology budgets is gone. MCP collapsed it. The domain knowledge required to build it still exists only in practitioners — in CPAs and controllers and auditors who understand not just the data but what the data means and what gets it wrong. That knowledge has not been commoditized. It cannot be downloaded. It accumulates over years of actual client work, and it is the one input that a general-purpose AI vendor cannot supply.

That combination — accessible infrastructure, scarce domain knowledge — defines a window. It will not stay open indefinitely. As MCP matures, as more vendors invest in domain-specific logic, as the large platforms begin to acquire the vertical tools that are being built today, the advantage that comes from moving first will compress. The firms and practitioners who build Tier 2 capability now, on their own terms, with their own domain knowledge embedded in the system, will have an asset that is very difficult to replicate from the outside.

Doempke's timeline is worth taking seriously. Speaking in March 2026, his assessment was direct: if you are a practitioner not changing your workflows, you have maybe twelve months before someone who embraced this passes you. Not because they are smarter. Because they stopped being the bottleneck. That is the version of this that does not make headlines — not the dramatic displacement story, but the quiet competitive erosion of firms that kept doing Tier 1 work manually while others automated it and moved up.

> *The question is not whether accounting AI will reach Tier 2 and Tier 3 at scale. It will. The question is whether your firm is building toward it or waiting to buy it from someone who did.*

Part One has given you the framework: three tiers, a diagnostic for placing any tool accurately on the map, the professional context that makes getting it right a requirement rather than a preference, and the infrastructure shift that makes it buildable now. Part Two uses that framework to audit your firm — workflow by workflow, decision by decision — so you can see exactly where you are, where the gaps are, and where to start.

CHAPTER 4

Where Most Firms Actually Are

> "Today it is no longer impressive for a firm to say it uses AI. What will be impressive are those firms who use AI to deliver measurable, explainable, and consistent results. 2025 was the year of AI experimentation; 2026 will be the year of accountability."
> — Accounting Today, 2026

Jody Padar — author of The Radical CPA and one of the accounting profession's most widely followed voices on firm innovation — described the adoption problem in a single image: a traffic jam. Leadership tells the firm to explore AI. The IT department begins a security evaluation. A committee forms to review vendors. Meanwhile, staff start using AI tools quietly on their own — because nobody told them it was allowed, and because the work still has to get done. The committee never finishes. The vendor evaluation drags. The staff experiments produce no institutional learning because nothing is being captured. The firm is simultaneously moving and standing still.

This is not a story about firms that do not want to change. It is a story about firms that want to change and cannot find the entry point. The conversation about AI in the profession has been dominated by two narratives that are both true and both unhelpful: the transformation narrative, which says AI will change everything and firms must act now; and the caution narrative, which says the risks are real and firms must move carefully. Both are correct. Neither tells a managing partner what to do on Monday morning.

The Innovation Traffic Jam

The traffic jam pattern is specific enough to be worth mapping precisely, because firms that recognize themselves in it can break out of it deliberately rather than waiting for the jam to clear on its own.

It typically starts with a directive from leadership — often prompted by a conference, a competitor announcement, or a vendor pitch — to explore how AI can be used in the firm. The directive is genuine. Leadership is not performing interest; they are genuinely uncertain and want someone to figure it out. But the directive lands in an organizational structure that was not designed to absorb it.

IT receives a security evaluation request. Legal reviews the vendor's terms of service. A working group forms, typically populated by the people who can be spared for committee work rather than the people closest to the workflows being evaluated. Vendors are invited to demo. The demos look impressive — and the committee, lacking the tier framework to evaluate what they are actually seeing, cannot distinguish between a system that will perform in production and one that performs in a controlled demonstration on clean data.

While this is happening, staff have not stopped working. They have started using AI tools — free consumer versions, because those are available immediately — to get through their workload. Some of these experiments are producing real efficiency gains. None of them are being captured. The staff member who figured out how to use AI to cut the first draft of a client memo from two hours to twenty minutes has not documented the workflow, has not shared it with colleagues, and is quietly hoping nobody asks whether they used AI because the policy does not exist yet.

> *The firm is generating institutional learning about AI every day. It is losing that learning every day because there is no system to capture it.*

The Karbon State of AI in Accounting report found that while most practitioners are using

AI in some form, structured firm-wide approaches remain the exception. The gap between individual experimentation and institutional adoption is not a technology problem. It is a capture problem. The learning exists. The infrastructure to absorb it does not.

Copilot First Is Correct. Copilot Only Is a Trap.

Part One established that most firms should start with Tier 1 — the pattern-matching, category-recognition work that requires no domain judgment and no deep data access. That is the right starting point. The question is what you build toward from there.

Sequoia Capital, in a published analysis of the AI services market, draws a precise distinction between two modes of AI deployment: the copilot, which sells the tool and keeps the professional in the loop; and the autopilot, which sells the work and routes around the professional entirely. Most accounting firms today are operating in copilot mode — not the Microsoft button in the Excel ribbon, but a posture: AI that accelerates Tier 1 workflows, assists the practitioner on routine tasks, and keeps the professional at the center of every output. That is the correct first move. It reduces risk, builds staff familiarity, and generates the institutional knowledge that makes the next layer possible.

The trap is treating copilot mode as the destination. A firm that deploys AI across its Tier 1 workflows, measures the efficiency gain, declares success, and stops has accomplished something real. It has also handed an advantage to the firms that kept building. Sequoia's analysis of the AI services market identified the underlying reason: for every dollar spent on software, six are spent on services — on the actual delivery of professional work. The copilot sells your firm a better way to deliver. The autopilot sells the delivery itself, directly to your client, at a price built on software margins rather than professional fees.

> *The copilot makes your firm more efficient. The autopilot makes your firm optional.*

Copilot deployment is the right first move. The question is what it prepares you to build next. The firms that use Tier 1 deployment to learn — about their data, their workflows, their clients, and their own domain logic — are the ones positioned to move into Tier 2 deliberately. That is where the defensible advantage lives: not in having AI, but in having AI that knows something specific about your clients that no horizontal platform is designed to know.

Skipping the Sequence

Some firms, impatient with the pace of Tier 1 gains, move directly toward agentic systems — AI that does not just assist but acts: posting journal entries, updating records, executing multi-step workflows without a human in each loop. The efficiency gains are real. So is the failure mode that opens when the tier sequence gets skipped.

An operator of an educational technology platform documented what happened when an AI coding agent was given access to infrastructure systems. The agent was instructed to clean up resources. It executed the command correctly. It destroyed the production database, the backups, and the entire cloud environment the platform ran on. Two and a half years of user data — homework, projects, leaderboards — was gone. The agent did not make an error in the conventional sense. It did exactly what it was asked to do. The problem was that it had no understanding of the consequences of being wrong about scope, and no instruction to stop and verify before acting.

The agent had pattern-matching confidence — it identified the task, executed the steps, and completed the operation. What it did not have was consequences knowledge: the understanding that "clean up" means something categorically different depending on whether you are in a test environment or a live one, and that the cost of being wrong about scope is not recoverable. A senior engineer would have paused. The agent did not, because nobody told it to.

> *The agent did not malfunction. It performed. The failure was in what was never built: an instruction to stop and ask before the consequences became irreversible.*

For accounting firms, the analog is direct. An AI agent with access to a client's general ledger, authorized to post journal entries, categorize transactions, and update records, is operating in a production environment where every action has downstream consequences. Into the financial statements. Into the tax return. Into the client's business decisions. The agent that categorizes a transaction incorrectly does not know it was incorrect. It does not flag the result for review. It moves to the next task with the same confidence it brought to the one it got wrong.

This is not an argument against agentic AI in accounting. Agentic systems are where the efficiency gains become transformative — the difference between AI that assists your workflow and AI that runs it. The argument is about sequence and design. Agentic access without judgment boundaries is not a more powerful copilot. It is a liability surface. The judgment boundary — the designed point at which the agent stops executing and routes a decision to a human — must be built before the access is granted, not after the first incident.

The technical infrastructure for building those boundaries exists. MCP-connected systems can be configured with explicit permission scopes that limit what an agent can access and act on. Workflow designs can include mandatory review gates for high-consequence actions — anything that touches a filed document, a client-facing output, or a record that feeds downstream reporting. Audit trails can log every agent action in terms a practitioner can review. None of this happens automatically. It requires deliberate design by someone who understands both the technology and the professional standards that govern the output.

The Cost of Standing Still

Firms that are waiting — for the technology to mature, for the profession's standards to clarify, for a competitor to go first and validate the path — are making a real choice with real costs. The costs are not always visible because they are costs of position rather than costs of action: the clients who do not ask for a proposal because they found someone who already has the capability, the staff who leave for a firm that is building something, the pricing pressure that arrives when a competitor can deliver the same work faster and charges accordingly.

The Sequoia analysis of the accounting and audit market places it squarely in what they call autopilot territory — outsourced, intelligence-heavy, with a structural talent shortage that is accelerating client willingness to accept AI-delivered work. Bloomberg data puts the number of accountants the profession has lost at roughly 340,000 over five years. That figure, combined with the demographic cliff of practitioners approaching retirement, is not creating job security. It is creating a vacuum that clients will fill with whatever is available. A well-funded startup does not need to be better than a good accountant. It needs to be available when a good accountant is not.

The firms most exposed are not the ones that have decided not to adopt AI. They are the firms that have adopted it at Tier 1 and stopped, while the market moves toward Tier 2 and 3 capability. Tier 1 adoption is now table stakes in most markets. It reduces costs but does not create differentiation, because every firm can deploy the same categorization engine, the same document processing layer, the same Tier 1 workflow automation. The competitive question is not whether you have AI in your stack. It is whether your AI knows something the next firm's AI does not.

> *Tier 1 adoption eliminates inefficiency. Tier 2 creates advantage. The firms that stop at Tier 1 have optimized a business model that is still exposed to the same competitive forces that were always coming.*

The profession's own data confirms where the gap is. The 2026 Karbon report found that a significant majority of practitioners believe AI will handle most Tier 1 tasks within a few years. The same practitioners overwhelmingly identify client advisory work — Tier 3 — as the function most resistant to AI displacement and most central to firm value. The gap between where AI is being deployed and where firm value actually lives is the map of the work that still needs to be done.

The Workflow Assessment

Most firms assume they know where they stand with AI. The vendor dashboard says adoption is high. The managing partner heard positive feedback from staff. A few workflows feel faster. None of that tells you what tier your firm is actually operating at, where the gaps are, or what the next move is. That is what the workflow assessment does: it maps how work actually moves through the firm, step by step, and puts a tier label on each step.

The starting point is always the gaps — the work that lives between your platforms and is currently being done by the most expensive resource in your firm: a trained professional acting as an integration layer between systems. Reading a client's bank statement and drafting the follow-up email about uncategorized transactions. Pulling numbers from the general ledger and writing the narrative paragraph for the monthly report. Building a meeting brief from prior workpapers, open items, and notes stored across three different systems. This work is Tier 1 in nature — it requires no domain judgment, just retrieval, synthesis, and formatting. It is being done manually because nobody has deployed the automation. The gap work is where every firm starts, and it is where the fastest ROI lives.

From there, the audit moves into the workflows where domain knowledge is actually required — where the question is not just what happened in the data, but what it means and what to do about it. These are the Tier 2 workflows: the review processes where a practitioner's judgment determines whether the AI's output is trusted or revised; the advisory conversations where a client's specific situation requires analysis that a general-purpose tool cannot provide; the compliance work where the difference between a categorization that is technically defensible and one that is actually correct depends on facts the system must be designed to ask for.

The assessment does not tell you to build everything at once. It tells you where you are and what the next move is. For most firms, the next move is filling the Tier 1 gaps — deploying automation in the spaces no vendor controls, capturing the institutional learning that is currently being generated and lost, and building the data foundation that Tier 2 requires. The firms that do this work systematically arrive at Tier 2 with clean data, documented workflows, and a staff that already understands what the AI can and cannot do. The firms that skip it arrive at Tier 2 with the same data problems they started with, pointed at a more expensive system.

> *The goal of the assessment is not to identify everything that needs to change. It is to identify the one workflow where the cost of the current approach is clearest and the path to improvement is most direct. Start there.*

What that workflow looks like in practice — client onboarding, transaction processing, review and sign-off, advisory delivery — is where the work of building an AI-ready firm actually begins. The tier framework tells you what to build toward. The assessment tells you where you stand. The distance between those two points is the opportunity. Most firms have not started. The ones that do start now arrive at Tier 2 with a head start that compounds.

CHAPTER 5

Client Intake and Document Collection

The firm bought the portal two years ago. The onboarding was smooth, the vendor demo was convincing, and the managing partner sent an email to the entire client list explaining the new system and asking everyone to upload their documents there from now on. A handful of clients complied. The rest kept sending emails. Some still fax.

So the firm now runs two intake tracks. The official one, which the portal represents, and the real one, which is whatever the client prefers. An admin checks the portal, checks the inbox, downloads attachments, renames files according to the firm's convention — when the convention is followed — and moves everything into the client folder. When the practitioner opens the file to begin work, they assume it is complete. Sometimes it is. Sometimes the February bank statement is missing and they do not find out until they are halfway through the reconciliation.

Every firm reading this has a version of this story. The details vary. The structure does not. Intake is the most manual, most inconsistent, and most underexamined workflow in the practice — and it is the one that determines whether everything downstream starts from a complete and accurate foundation or from a guess.

Why Intake Is Harder Than It Looks

Intake looks simple from the outside. Documents come in. Documents get filed. Work begins. The complexity is in the gap between what comes in and what is actually needed — and in the fact that gap is invisible until it causes a problem.

The gap has three parts. The first is channel fragmentation. Clients send documents through whatever is easiest for them: email, the portal if they use it, a shared drive link, a text message with a photo of a paper document, occasionally a fax. Each channel requires a different retrieval step, a different handling process, and a different failure mode when something goes wrong. The firm that has ten clients using ten different delivery methods has ten intake workflows, not one.

The second part is document identification. A PDF attachment named "statement.pdf" is not self-describing. An admin who opens it learns what it is. An admin processing forty documents before noon makes reasonable assumptions and occasionally gets one wrong. The wrong assumption — last year's statement filed as this year's, a document for one entity filed under another, a corrected 1099 that supersedes the original but both get filed as current — does not announce itself. It waits.

The third part is completeness. Knowing that documents arrived is not the same as knowing that the right documents arrived. A client with three bank accounts should submit three statements. A client with rental income should submit a 1099 for each property that generated one. A client whose situation changed this year — a new entity, a refinancing, a property sold mid-year — has a different document set than last year, and the checklist from last year will not catch what is missing. Completeness verification is almost entirely manual in most practices today. It depends on a practitioner or admin who knows the client well enough to know what should be there.

> *The portal did not solve the intake problem. It added a channel. The intake problem is not about where documents arrive. It is about what happens to them after.*

The Tier Map for Intake

Applying the tier framework to intake reveals that the workflow divides cleanly along the same lines as every other workflow in the practice — and that most firms are operating at Tier 1 in a workflow where the cost of those limitations is paid downstream, not at intake itself.

Tier 1 intake receives and routes. It handles the logistics of document collection: retrieving files from whatever channel they arrive through, naming them according to a convention, placing them in the correct folder. This is the work currently done by admins, and it is the work that most practice management platforms — the portals, the document management systems, the email integrations — partially automate. A system that watches an inbox and moves attachments to a client folder is operating at Tier 1. It is handling the obvious part of the problem, faster and more consistently than a human doing the same task. That is real value. It is not complete.

Tier 2 intake understands what arrived. It opens the document, identifies what it is, verifies that it covers the expected period, checks whether it is a duplicate or a superseding version of something already in the file, and flags discrepancies before work begins. A Tier 2 intake system does not just move the file named "statement.pdf" into the client folder. It reads the file, confirms it is a bank statement for the correct account, confirms it covers the correct month, notes that a statement for this account covering this period already exists in the folder and flags the conflict for review. It does this for every document, for every client, every time — without variation and without requiring the person handling it to already know what should be there.

Tier 3 intake is proactive about completeness. It knows what each client's file should contain based on their entity structure, their prior year documents, and any changes in their situation that have been recorded. It generates a dynamic checklist at the start of each engagement period, tracks what has arrived against that checklist in real time, and surfaces the gap before the practitioner opens the file to begin work. Not "documents received" as a status indicator. "Three of seven required documents received — missing: Q4 bank statement for account ending 4471, 1099-NEC from Vendor A, and updated Schedule K-1 from Partnership B." The practitioner knows what they have before they discover what they do not.

> *No system on the market today performs Tier 2 intake at scale for accounting practices. Completeness verification is still manual, still inconsistent, and still the most common reason work gets interrupted after it has already started.*

Why the Portal Failed

The client portal is a Tier 1 solution to a problem that requires Tier 2 thinking. It consolidates the channel — documents arrive in one place instead of several — but it does not solve the identification problem or the completeness problem. And it introduces a new one: friction on the client side that the firm absorbs as a support burden.

Clients do not default to portals because portals are not where their documents already live. Their bank statements come by email. Their 1099s arrive in the mail or through their brokerage's website. Their lease agreements are in their inbox or on their phone. Asking a client to download a document from one place and upload it to another is asking them to add a step to a process they have already completed. Most clients will not do it — not because they are uncooperative but because it is easier not to, and email has always worked before.

The right frame for intake is not: how do we get clients onto the portal? It is: how do we build intelligence on the firm's side that works with however clients actually send documents? A system that watches the firm's email, identifies attachments from known clients, extracts document metadata, routes files to the correct folder, flags duplicates, and updates a completeness checklist does not require the client to change their behavior at all. The firm gets Tier 2 intake capability. The client sends an email the way they always have. That is the design the workflow actually needs.

Where AI Helps — and Where It Creates New Problems

AI is well-suited to document identification and routing. A system built on current AI infrastructure can read a PDF, identify that it is a bank statement for a specific account covering a specific period, and route it to the correct client folder with the correct naming convention applied — consistently, at scale, without variation. Firms that build this stop losing hours to manual filing during busy season and stop discovering mid-engagement that the wrong document was filed under the right client.

AI is also well-suited to duplicate and version detection. A system that has indexed the existing contents of a client folder can compare an incoming document against what is already there and flag when the same document arrived twice, when a corrected version supersedes an original already in the file, or when a document covers a period that overlaps with one already present. This is pattern matching across document metadata — exactly what Tier 1 AI handles reliably.

Where AI creates new problems is at the completeness gap. A system that confirms receipt of documents without verifying completeness produces a new kind of false confidence — the same confidence problem that applies to categorization, applied one step earlier in the workflow. If the intake system marks a client's file as "received" because documents arrived, but does not verify that the right documents arrived, the practitioner inherits an incomplete file wrapped in a status indicator that suggests otherwise. The system reported accurately that documents were received. It did not know what should have been received, so it could not report on what was missing.

The fix is not avoiding AI in intake. It is designing the completeness check before deploying the receipt confirmation. The system needs to know what each client's complete file looks like before it can report whether the file is complete. That knowledge has to be built and maintained — a per-client document checklist that reflects the client's current situation, updated when their circumstances change. Building that checklist is practitioner work. Running the completeness check against it, every engagement period, for every client, is the system's job.

Applying the Assessment to This Workflow

The workflow assessment for intake asks five questions. They are operational, not strategic. The answers identify exactly where manual work is concentrated and where the highest-leverage automation opportunity is.

The first question: how many channels does your firm currently receive documents through? Count them honestly — the portal, email, shared drives, text, fax, walk-ins during busy season. Each channel is a separate intake workflow. The number defines the scope of the consolidation problem before anything else is solved.

The second question: who currently performs document identification and filing, and how long does it take per client per engagement period? This is the Tier 1 automation target. If the answer is an admin spending two to four hours per client during busy season on filing and renaming alone, the case for Tier 1 intake automation is straightforward. The time is recoverable and the task is automatable today.

The third question: does your firm maintain a per-client document checklist, and who is responsible for verifying completeness before work begins? If the answer is no formal checklist — or yes, but it lives in someone's head — completeness verification is not a workflow step. It is a dependency on institutional knowledge that does not transfer when the person who holds it is unavailable. That dependency is the intake risk that most often interrupts work downstream.

The fourth question: how does your firm currently handle duplicate or superseded documents? If the answer is manually — someone checks before filing — that is a Tier 1 automation opportunity with a clear failure mode when the check is skipped. A corrected 1099 filed alongside the original rather than replacing it will produce an error downstream. The system can catch this consistently. Right now it relies on a human to remember.

The fifth question: at what point in your intake workflow do you first touch the file? In most firms the answer is: when they are ready to begin work. That is too late to catch an incomplete file without disrupting the engagement. You should not be the completeness check. The completeness check should happen before the file reaches you — so that when you open it, you are beginning work, not beginning discovery.

> *The most expensive intake failure is not the document that never arrived. It is the document that arrived, was filed, and was assumed to be sufficient — until the practitioner discovered otherwise mid-engagement.*

Where to Start

The intake workflow has two distinct automation layers and they should be built in order. The first is channel consolidation and document routing — the Tier 1 work. A system that watches the firm's email inbox, identifies attachments from known clients, extracts document metadata, and routes files to the correct folder with the correct naming convention is deployable today without replacing any existing infrastructure. It connects what already exists: the email system, the document management folder, and an AI layer that can read and classify PDFs. This recovers administrative hours immediately and is the right place to start.

The second layer is completeness verification — the Tier 2 work. This requires building the per-client document checklist first. Start with the clients whose intake is most complex: multiple entities, multiple account types, prior-year situations that created non-standard document requirements. Document what a complete file looks like for each of those clients. That documentation is what the completeness check runs against. Once it exists, the system compares incoming documents against the checklist in real time and flags the gap before work begins.

The clients who email will keep emailing. The clients who fax will keep faxing. The intelligence is on the firm's side. A system that meets clients where they are and builds completeness verification behind the scenes does not require anyone to change their behavior. It requires the firm to treat intake as the first professional judgment call of every engagement: does this file contain what it needs to contain before work begins? That question has always had to be answered. The only thing that changes is who answers it, when, and with what consistency.

CHAPTER 6

Bookkeeping, Classification, and the Judgment Line

The file looks good. That is the first thing you notice. Reconciled. Organized. Zero uncategorized transactions. The AI bookkeeping service your client signed up for has been running every month, and from the outside, it looks exactly like what you would want a clean set of books to look like.

You are twenty minutes into your review when you find it. A transaction type the system has been miscategorizing since the account was set up. Not randomly — consistently. The same merchant, the same amount range, the same wrong bucket, every single month for eight months. The system was not confused. It was confident. It applied the same logic every time and produced the same result every time, and because the output looked clean, nobody looked closely enough to catch it.

The consequence depends on what the transaction was. If it was a repair that should have been capitalized, the depreciation schedule is wrong and the tax return needs to be amended. If it was a mixed-use expense that needed allocation, the deduction is either overstated or understated and the client has an exposure they do not know about. If it was a payment to a vendor who should have received a 1099, the filing deadline may have already passed.

This is not a story about a system that failed. It is a story about a system that performed exactly as designed — and about the difference between a system that processes transactions and a practitioner who understands what they mean.

What Transaction Processing Actually Is

Transaction processing is the foundation of everything a firm produces. Before a tax return can be prepared, before a financial statement can be issued, before an advisory conversation can happen, the transactions have to be right. Not approximately right. Not right on average. Right in the specific cases where being wrong has consequences — which, in accounting, is most of them.

The workflow breaks into four stages that are worth naming precisely, because each stage has a different tier profile and a different failure mode.

The first stage is ingestion — getting transaction data from wherever it lives into a system where it can be worked. Bank feeds, credit card imports, vendor bills, payroll exports, expense reports. Most firms have automated significant portions of this stage already. It is the most mature part of the AI accounting stack and the least controversial. The technology is reliable, the error rate is low, and the failure mode when it does go wrong is usually visible: a missing feed, a duplicate import, a connection that dropped.

The second stage is categorization — assigning each transaction to the correct account, class, and dimension. This is where most AI accounting products compete, and where most of the marketing claims live. It is also where the tier framework becomes essential, because categorization looks like a solved problem until you understand what "correct" actually requires.

The third stage is review — a practitioner examining the categorized output, identifying what the system got wrong, and making the corrections that require judgment. This stage is where most firms underinvest, because it does not feel like a workflow step. It feels like checking. The difference matters: a workflow step is designed, documented, and executed consistently. Checking is informal, inconsistent, and the first thing that gets compressed when the deadline moves.

The fourth stage is close and sign-off — the practitioner's affirmative decision that the period's transactions are complete, accurate, and ready to support downstream work. This is the liability moment. Everything before it is preparation. This is the act.

The Tier Map for Transaction Processing

Applying the tier framework to transaction processing produces a map that most firms will find uncomfortable, because it makes visible something that is easier to leave unexamined: the system your firm currently relies on for categorization is almost certainly operating at Tier 1, and Tier 1 is not enough for the work you are signing.

Tier 1 categorization knows patterns. It has seen enough transactions to recognize that charges from hardware stores tend to be repairs, that charges from staffing agencies tend to be contract labor, that charges from insurance carriers tend to be insurance expense. It applies those patterns confidently and consistently. For the majority of transactions in a typical client file — the ones that are exactly what they appear to be — it is right.

What Tier 1 does not know is consequences. It does not know that the client's written capitalization policy sets a threshold below which repairs are expensed and above which they are capitalized — and that the $4,200 hardware store charge crossed that threshold. It does not know that the same vendor appears on both the personal and business accounts, and that the business charge this month was actually a personal expense run through the wrong card. It does not know that the payment categorized as rent is actually a lease payment that triggers

ASC 842 disclosure obligations. It categorizes what it sees. It does not know what it cannot see.

> *Tier 1 is right about most transactions. The problem is that the transactions it gets wrong are rarely the ones that cost the least to fix.*

Tier 2 transaction processing knows consequences. It applies domain knowledge to categorization decisions: what does this transaction imply for the tax return? Does this expense pattern suggest a classification issue the practitioner should review? Does this vendor relationship require disclosure? The difference between Tier 1 and Tier 2 in this workflow is not accuracy on routine transactions — both tiers handle those well. The difference is what happens at the edges, where the transaction requires context that is not visible in the transaction itself.

Tier 3 in transaction processing is proactive. It surfaces the question before the practitioner thinks to ask it. Not "this transaction needs review" but "this client's repair spend over the past three months has crossed the threshold where a cost segregation analysis changes the tax outcome — flag for partner discussion before the return is prepared." The transaction is the signal. The insight is what the system does with it.

Where Most Firms Actually Sit

Most firms are running a Tier 1 categorization engine and a Tier 3 review expectation. The system processes. You are expected to catch everything the system missed. That gap — between what the automation actually does and what the sign-off implicitly guarantees — is where the liability lives.

The review step in most firms is not designed to catch Tier 1 failures systematically. It is designed to spot obvious errors. A practitioner scanning a categorized file is looking for things that look wrong. The problem the opening scenario describes — consistent miscategorization that produces clean-looking output — does not look wrong. It looks right. Catching it requires knowing what to look for, which requires either domain knowledge applied to a specific review protocol or a system designed to flag the categories where Tier 1 confidence is least reliable.

This is not a criticism of the practitioners doing the review. It is a description of a structural mismatch between the tool and the task. Tier 1 systems are not designed to signal their own uncertainty. They do not produce output that says "I categorized this as repairs, but given the amount and the client's history, a practitioner should verify." They produce output that says: repairs. The uncertainty is invisible, which means the review step has to supply what the tool does not.

> *The risk in transaction processing is not that the system makes obvious mistakes. It is that the system makes confident ones.*

What Tier 2 Looks Like in This Workflow

A Tier 2 transaction processing system does not replace the practitioner's review. It changes what the review is for. Instead of scanning output for obvious errors, the practitioner is reviewing flagged exceptions — the transactions the system identified as requiring judgment that the categorization engine cannot supply.

The flags are not random. They are generated by logic that knows what the system does not know. A repair-versus-capital-improvement flag triggers when a charge to a contractor or building supply vendor exceeds the client's capitalization threshold and the asset has not been confirmed as existing inventory. A mixed-use flag triggers when the same expense category appears on both personal and business feeds for the same client. A reclassification flag triggers when a payment pattern suggests the categorization applied last month no longer matches the facts this month. Each flag is a question the system cannot answer but knows enough to ask.

The practitioner reviews the flags, not the file. That is the structural shift. In a Tier 1 workflow, review time scales with transaction volume — more transactions, more time. In a Tier 2 workflow, review time scales with exception volume, which is a much smaller number. The practitioner's time goes to the decisions that require their judgment. The system handles the rest and documents that it did.

The documentation is not incidental. It is part of what makes the output signable. A workpaper that shows not just what the transactions were categorized as, but which ones were flagged, which were reviewed, and what determination was made, is a fundamentally different artifact than a categorized ledger. The first is a processed file. The second is evidence of professional judgment applied to a processed file. Courts, auditors, and regulators treat them differently. So do professional liability insurers.

Applying the Assessment to This Workflow

The workflow assessment for transaction processing asks four questions. They are not complicated, but most firms have never asked them explicitly, which is why the answers are often surprising.

The first question: what tier is your categorization engine operating at? If your system categorizes transactions without flagging exceptions based on client-specific rules or consequence logic, it is operating at Tier 1. That is not a failure — it is an accurate description of what most systems are designed to do. Knowing it is Tier 1 tells you what the review step has to supply.

The second question: what is your review step actually designed to catch? If the answer is "obvious errors," the review step is not designed to catch Tier 1 failures. It needs either a protocol that targets the categories where Tier 1 is least reliable, or a system layer that flags those categories before review begins.

The third question: where does client-specific knowledge live in your current workflow? Capitalization policies, mixed-use ratios, recurring vendor relationships that require special treatment, passive activity rules that apply to this client's specific entity structure — is that knowledge documented in a system that can be applied at categorization time, or does it live in a practitioner's head and get applied inconsistently at review time? If it is in a head, it is not a workflow. It is a dependency.

The fourth question: what does your sign-off actually certify? Most practitioners would answer: that the transactions are correctly categorized. The more precise answer is: that a trained professional reviewed the output of a Tier 1 system and applied judgment to the exceptions they were able to identify. That is a different statement. Knowing which one you are making is the difference between a defensible position and an exposed one.

> *The sign-off is not the end of the workflow. It is the accountability moment. Everything before it is preparation for what the signature means.*

Where to Start

Firms that want to move transaction processing toward Tier 2 do not need to replace their current system. They need to add the layer their current system does not have: the client-specific rules and consequences that turns categorization confidence into categorization accuracy.

The practical starting point is the exception list. For each client, identify the transaction categories where your current system is least reliable — where you have caught errors in the past, where the rules are client-specific rather than general, where a miscategorization has downstream consequences that are expensive to fix. That list is the first version of a Tier 2 flag protocol. It does not require new software. It requires documenting what an experienced practitioner already knows and building it into the review process as a consistent check rather than an occasional catch.

From there, the question is which of those exceptions can be systematized — encoded into rules that the categorization layer can apply before the transaction reaches the review step. Some can. The capitalization threshold is a rule. The mixed-use allocation ratio is a rule. The vendor relationship that always requires reclassification is a rule. Rules that can be encoded should be. The practitioner's time is too valuable to spend catching the same thing every month.

What cannot be encoded is judgment about novel situations — the transaction type you have not seen before, the client circumstance that changed since last quarter, the regulatory development that shifts how a category should be treated. That is what the review step is for. Not checking the obvious. Handling the new. That is Tier 2 work, and it is the work that justifies the signature.

The firms that build this layer are not just reducing their liability exposure. They are building the data foundation that makes every downstream workflow more reliable — the tax return that does not require three rounds of corrections, the financial statement that does not surface surprises at review, the advisory conversation that starts from numbers the client can trust. Transaction processing is not the most visible work a firm does. It is the work that determines whether everything else is worth doing.

CHAPTER 7

Workpaper Prep and Review Workflows

The workpaper package looks good. Formatted consistently, cross-referenced correctly, the math checks out. The senior manager opens it expecting to spend an hour on review and finds herself moving faster than usual — the AI-prepared workpapers are cleaner than what the staff used to produce, the tie-outs are complete, and nothing obvious is missing.

Halfway through, she slows down. Not because she found an error. Because she realizes she has been reviewing the workpapers the same way she always has — checking formatting, verifying math, confirming that numbers tie to the source. And those things are fine. But the AI already checked them. She is auditing the AI's arithmetic, which the AI does not get wrong, while the questions that actually require her judgment — whether the classification is defensible, whether the client's position is consistent with last year, whether there is an issue here that needs disclosure — are embedded in the narrative sections she has been skimming because they look complete.

She has been reviewing the output. She has not been reviewing the judgment.

This is not a story about a bad reviewer. It is a story about a review process designed for human-prepared work being applied without modification to AI-prepared work. The format is the same. The checklist is the same. What changed is what the preparer actually did — and what the reviewer actually needs to supply. Nobody redesigned the review to match.

What Workpaper Review Is Actually For

Workpaper review has always had two distinct functions that most firms treat as one. The first is quality control — verifying that the work was done correctly, that the numbers are accurate, that the documentation is complete, and that the output meets the firm's standards. The second is professional judgment — confirming that the positions taken are defensible, that the conclusions are appropriate given the client's specific facts, and that nothing requires escalation, disclosure, or a different treatment than what the preparer selected.

When a human prepares a workpaper, quality control and professional judgment are intertwined. The reviewer checks the math and in doing so evaluates whether the approach was right. They verify the tie-out and in doing so assess whether the correct source document was used. The two functions happen simultaneously because the reviewer cannot verify the output without engaging with the decisions that produced it.

When AI prepares a workpaper, those two functions separate. Quality control — accuracy, completeness, formatting, internal consistency — is something AI does reliably and at a level that exceeds most human preparers. Reviewing it manually is not where a senior practitioner's time creates value. Professional judgment — whether the position is right, whether the facts support it, whether there is something here that deserves a different conclusion — is something AI does not supply and cannot supply. That is where the reviewer's time belongs.

> *In a human-prepared workpaper, quality control and professional judgment are inseparable. In an AI-prepared workpaper, they have to be deliberately separated — because the reviewer who checks both equally is wasting the time that only they can spend.*

The Tier Map for Workpaper Prep

Workpaper preparation divides along the tier framework as cleanly as any workflow in the practice. Understanding where each component sits tells you which parts AI should own, which parts require practitioner involvement, and where the judgment line actually falls.

Tier 1 workpaper preparation is the structural work: pulling data from the source systems, populating the standard schedules, performing the mathematical calculations, applying the firm's formatting conventions, generating the cross-reference index, and flagging any items that do not reconcile. This work is rules-based, repeatable, and verifiable. A system that does it correctly every time — without transposition errors, without missed tie-outs, without inconsistent formatting between sections — produces a workpaper package that is more reliable at the structural level than most human-prepared packages. The value of Tier 1 workpaper prep is not incremental efficiency. It is structural reliability at a level humans cannot sustain at volume.

Tier 2 workpaper preparation encodes the judgment that experienced practitioners apply routinely but rarely document. It knows that a specific client's entity structure means a particular schedule needs an additional disclosure. It knows that a transaction type appearing this year for the first time requires a classification decision that should be documented with a supporting rationale, not just categorized and moved past. It knows that the comparison to prior year should flag a variance that exceeds the firm's materiality threshold and route it to the reviewer's attention with the prior year context already assembled. Tier 2 preparation does not just produce the workpaper. It surfaces what the reviewer needs to engage with before the reviewer opens the file.

Tier 3 workpaper preparation is proactive. It identifies the issue the practitioner has not thought to look for yet. It connects a pattern across multiple schedules that individually look unremarkable but together suggest a position that needs to be examined. It surfaces the planning opportunity that the current year's workpapers reveal but that requires action before the filing date, not after. A Tier 3 system does not wait for the reviewer to ask the question. It asks the question first and documents why it was asked.

Most AI workpaper preparation today operates at Tier 1, with some firms beginning to build Tier 2 logic into their systems. Tier 3 exists in isolated examples but has not been productized at scale for accounting practices. The implication is practical: if your current AI workpaper system is operating at Tier 1, your review process needs to supply everything Tier 2 and Tier 3 would have provided. That means the reviewer is not just approving quality-controlled output. They are doing the Tier 2 judgment work that the preparation system did not do.

Why the Old Review Process Does Not Fit

The traditional workpaper review process was designed around a specific assumption: that the preparer made judgment calls throughout the work and that the reviewer's job was to evaluate those calls. The tick marks, the sign-offs, the review notes — all of it was built to document that a qualified professional examined the decisions another qualified professional made.

AI preparation breaks that assumption in a specific way. The AI did not make judgment calls. It applied rules. Where it had rules, it applied them consistently. Where it did not have rules, it either left the item unresolved or made a default decision that may or may not be appropriate for this client. The reviewer applying the traditional review process to AI output is looking for judgment calls that were never made — which means they are not finding them, which means the actual judgment questions are getting reviewed at the same level as the formatting.

There is a second problem. Traditional review processes treat all sections of a workpaper roughly equally — the reviewer moves through the package in order, spending time proportional to the length of each section. AI-prepared workpapers invert this. The sections that are longest and most detailed are often the ones where AI performed best: the data schedules, the mathematical summaries, the reconciliations. The sections that require the most professional judgment are often the shortest: the classification rationale, the position documentation, the disclosure analysis. A review process that allocates time proportionally to length will spend most of its time on the least valuable review work.

> *The review process that worked for human-prepared workpapers is not wrong. It is misaligned. It was built to catch human errors. AI-prepared workpapers have a different error profile — and the review has to match it.*

What a Redesigned Review Looks Like

A review process designed for AI-prepared workpapers starts by separating what the reviewer does not need to verify from what only the reviewer can determine. That separation is the foundation of an efficient review in an AI-assisted practice.

The first layer of the redesigned review is exception-based, not comprehensive. The AI flags what it could not resolve, what fell outside the rules it was given, and what produced a result that differs materially from prior periods without an explanation already in the file. The reviewer engages with those flags first. They are the items where the AI stopped and where the practitioner's judgment is the only thing that moves the work forward. Everything else — the items the AI resolved within its rules — gets reviewed at a lower level of scrutiny, with the reviewer confirming that the rule was applied correctly rather than re-evaluating whether the output is right.

The second layer is judgment-focused, not mechanics-focused. The reviewer's attention goes to the classification rationale, the position documentation, and the disclosure analysis — the sections where professional judgment determines the answer, not arithmetic. Those sections should be longer and more detailed in AI-prepared workpapers than they were in human-prepared ones, because the AI's job includes surfacing the questions it cannot answer and documenting the context the reviewer needs to engage with them. A well-designed AI workpaper preparation system does not just produce the schedules. It prepares the reviewer.

The third layer is documented. The review is not complete when the reviewer has mentally concluded that the work is right. It is complete when the reviewer has documented which items were flagged, which required their judgment, and what determination was made on each. That documentation is not bureaucratic overhead. It is the evidence that a licensed professional exercised judgment over AI output — which is the professional and legal standard that the signature on the workpaper represents. Courts and professional liability insurers are increasingly asking not just whether a human reviewed AI output, but whether the review was substantive. Documented judgment is the answer to that question.

The fourth layer is calibrated to risk. Not every client file carries the same review burden. A straightforward engagement for a client whose situation has not changed materially from prior year, whose transactions are clean, and whose AI-flagged exceptions are few warrants a lighter review than a complex engagement with a new entity, a significant transaction, or a first-time position. The review process should be designed to modulate intensity based on the AI's own assessment of the file's complexity — which is information the system already has if it was designed to surface it.

Applying the Assessment to This Workflow

The workflow assessment for workpaper prep and review asks four questions. They are diagnostic questions about the current state of the review process, not aspirational questions about what it should become. The answers reveal whether the review is functioning as a professional judgment exercise or as a quality control check on a process that already quality-controls itself.

The first question: does your current review process distinguish between items the AI resolved and items the AI flagged for judgment? If the reviewer moves through the workpaper package in order without a separate treatment for flagged items, the review is comprehensive but not calibrated. The items that most need judgment are getting the same attention as the items that need none.

The second question: does your AI workpaper preparation system surface the questions it could not answer? A preparation system that produces clean output without flagging its own uncertainty is not a Tier 2 system. It is a Tier 1 system in a Tier 2 format. The reviewer cannot engage with judgment questions the system did not surface. If the flags are not there, the review process has to supply them — which means the reviewer is doing the preparation system's job.

The third question: what does your current review documentation record? If the answer is sign-offs and tick marks, the documentation records that a review occurred. It does not record what the reviewer evaluated, what judgment was applied, or what the reviewer concluded about the items that required their expertise. That distinction matters when a position is challenged — by a client, an auditor, or a regulator. Sign-offs document presence. Documented judgment documents the work.

The fourth question: has your review time gone up or down since introducing AI workpaper preparation — and do you know why? If review time went down significantly, the most likely explanation is that the reviewer is spending less time on the items that require their judgment, not more. Efficiency in review is not automatically a good sign. A review that takes less time because it is more focused is an improvement. A review that takes less time because the reviewer skimmed the judgment sections is a liability.

> *The signature on a workpaper has always meant the same thing: a licensed professional reviewed this work and stands behind it. AI did not change what the signature means. It changed what the reviewer has to do to earn it.*

Where to Start

The starting point for redesigning workpaper review is an honest assessment of what the current AI preparation system actually flags. Pull three recent workpaper packages prepared by AI and examine them the way a reviewer would. Identify every item the system surfaced as requiring judgment. Count them. Then ask: are those the right items? Are there classification questions, position questions, or disclosure questions in those packages that the system did not flag but that a senior practitioner would have paused on?

The gap between what the system flagged and what an experienced practitioner would have flagged is the map of what the review process has to supply. If the gap is small, the preparation system is doing Tier 2 work well and the review process primarily needs to be redesigned for efficiency — more time on the flags, less time on the resolved items. If the gap is large, the preparation system is doing Tier 1 work and the review process is carrying the full weight of professional judgment without being designed for it.

From there, the practical build is a flag protocol — a defined set of conditions under which the preparation system is required to surface an item for reviewer judgment rather than resolve it. Conditions that belong in a flag protocol include: any transaction that exceeds a materiality threshold without a prior-year equivalent; any classification that does not have an established rule and requires a new determination; any position that differs from how the same item was treated in the prior year; any item that touches a disclosure question the system was not designed to resolve. The flag protocol does not replace the reviewer's judgment. It ensures the reviewer's judgment is applied where it is actually needed.

The firms that build this layer are not just reducing review time. They are building something more durable: a documented record of professional judgment applied to AI output, engagement by engagement, that compounds into an institutional standard for what review means in an AI-assisted practice. That standard is what the profession will eventually formalize. The firms that build it now will not be adapting to the standard. They will have been practicing it.

CHAPTER 8

The Prioritization Matrix

By this point in the assessment, you have the same problem most firms reach. You have seen enough to know that multiple workflows need attention. Intake is fragmented. Transaction processing relies on a Tier 1 engine that your review process was not designed to catch. Workpaper review has not been redesigned for AI-prepared output. The gap between where your firm is and where it needs to be is visible — and it is larger than one quarter's capacity to address.

The answer is not to address everything at once. The answer is to identify the first move that makes the second move possible — the change that creates the most forward momentum given what the firm actually has available to spend, both in time and in tolerance for disruption. That is what the prioritization matrix does. It does not tell you what the optimal long-term AI strategy looks like. It tells you where to start, and why starting there is better than starting anywhere else.

Why Prioritization Usually Fails

Most firms that get stuck after the assessment stage get stuck the same way. They evaluate potential AI initiatives by a single dimension — usually impact, because impact is the most visible — and they select the initiative with the highest projected return. That initiative turns out to be more complex than anticipated, encounters resistance, stalls, and the firm learns nothing useful from the failure except that AI implementation is hard.

The problem is not that the high-impact initiative was wrong. It is that impact without readiness is a plan for a firm you do not yet have. The initiative that produces the most value for a firm with clean data, documented workflows, staff trained on AI output, and a functional review process is not the same initiative that produces the most value for a firm that has none of those things. Prioritization has to account for where you are, not just where the initiative would take you.

The three dimensions that matter for prioritization are impact, risk, and readiness. Each one is independently important. All three together produce a ranking that a firm can actually execute — not just approve and then stall on.

The Three Dimensions

Impact measures what changes if the initiative succeeds. This is not just time saved — it includes error rate reduction, liability exposure reduction, capacity recovered for higher-tier work, and client experience improvement. A Tier 1 automation that saves four hours per client per engagement period across forty clients is recovering 160 hours that can be redirected to advisory work. That is real impact. But so is a Tier 2 flag protocol that catches the miscategorization that would have cost a client a $12,000 tax position. Impact has multiple currencies. The matrix scores all of them.

Risk measures what can go wrong. In AI implementation, risk has three common forms. Execution risk is the probability that the initiative does not get built or deployed as intended — because the technology is unfamiliar, the vendor relationship is uncertain, or the internal capacity to manage the change is limited. Output risk is the probability that the system produces incorrect results that reach a client before a practitioner catches them — which, in an accounting context, means incorrect tax positions, incorrect financial statements, or incorrect advice. Adoption risk is the probability that staff and clients do not use the system as designed, producing a parallel workflow problem rather than a solved one. Each form of risk matters differently depending on the initiative.

Readiness measures what the firm actually has available to execute. This is the most honest and most frequently skipped dimension in prioritization. Readiness has four components: data readiness (is the underlying data clean enough for the system to use reliably?), workflow readiness (is the current workflow documented well enough to encode into a system?), staff readiness (does the team understand what the system will and will not do, and can they review its output competently?), and capacity readiness (is there time and budget available to implement and maintain the change without disrupting current-season commitments?). A firm that scores low on readiness for a high-impact initiative should not skip the initiative — it should build readiness first, deliberately, before attempting the initiative.

> *The right first move is not the highest-impact initiative. It is the highest-impact initiative your firm is actually ready to execute. Those are rarely the same thing — and confusing them is how AI programs stall.*

Scoring the Matrix

The matrix works by scoring each candidate initiative on all three dimensions and using the combined score to rank order the starting sequence. The scoring does not require precision — it requires honesty. A high, medium, or low rating on each dimension is sufficient to produce a useful ranking. The goal is not a mathematically optimal answer. It is a defensible starting point that the firm's leadership can commit to without revisiting every quarter.

High impact, low risk, high readiness: start here. This is the initiative that recovers meaningful capacity, is unlikely to produce errors that reach clients, and can be executed with what the firm currently has. These initiatives are often in the Tier 1 automation category — document routing, intake consolidation, gap-work automation between platforms. They are not glamorous. They are the foundation everything else builds on.

High impact, high risk, high readiness: start second. These initiatives produce significant value but require careful design — particularly around output risk. A Tier 2 categorization system with a flag protocol falls here for most firms. The readiness has to be genuine before this initiative begins: the client-specific rules need to be documented, the review process needs to be redesigned, and the staff needs to understand what they are reviewing before the system goes live.

High impact, any risk, low readiness: build readiness first. Do not attempt this initiative yet. Instead, identify the specific readiness gap — data quality, workflow documentation, staff familiarity, capacity — and address it deliberately. The initiative stays on the roadmap. It moves to a later quarter when the readiness condition is met.

Low impact, low risk, high readiness: consider it only if it builds a capability you need for a higher-impact initiative. Document routing is low-impact in isolation but high-value as the foundation for Tier 2 intake. A Tier 1 automation that recovers thirty minutes per client per week is low-impact at the individual level but meaningful at the portfolio level if the firm has fifty clients. Context matters.

Low impact, high risk, any readiness: defer or eliminate. An initiative that is unlikely to produce meaningful value and carries significant execution or output risk is not a learning opportunity. It is a distraction. The firm's limited implementation capacity is better spent elsewhere.

The Readiness Condition in Practice

The readiness dimension deserves more attention than it typically receives, because it is where most firms are surprised by their own position. A firm that believes it is ready to implement a Tier 2 categorization system will often discover, on honest examination, that it cannot answer three of the four readiness questions satisfactorily.

Data readiness is almost always the first problem. AI systems are reliable when the data they work with is clean, complete, and consistently structured. Most firms' transaction data is not. Bank feeds have gaps. Document names are inconsistent. Prior-year workpapers are stored in formats that a system cannot read without conversion. The firm that tries to implement a Tier 2 intelligence layer on top of Tier 0 data infrastructure will spend most of its implementation time cleaning data rather than building the intelligence layer. That is not a system failure. It is a sequencing failure.

Workflow readiness is the second common gap. A workflow that lives in a practitioner's head cannot be encoded into a system. It has to be documented first — every step, every decision point, every exception that gets handled differently depending on the client. That documentation work is not glamorous and it does not feel like AI implementation. It is the prerequisite for AI implementation that most firms skip and then wonder why the system does not behave the way they expected.

Staff readiness is the third. A team that does not understand what an AI system is doing, or what its limitations are, cannot review its output effectively. Chapter 7 described the senior manager reviewing AI-prepared workpapers the same way she reviewed human-prepared workpapers — spending time where no time was needed and skimming where all the judgment lived. That failure is a staff readiness failure. The solution is not a training program. It is deliberate exposure: the staff needs to see the system produce correct output, incorrect output, and uncertain output before they can calibrate their review appropriately.

> *Readiness is not a prerequisite to check off before the real work begins. Building readiness is the real work. The firm that builds it deliberately arrives at implementation with a system that works. The firm that skips it arrives at implementation twice.*

The Matrix in Practice

Consider a mid-size practice with thirty-five active clients, two senior practitioners, and one administrative staff member. The assessment revealed three priority candidates: an email-based intake automation that routes documents and flags completeness gaps, a Tier 2 categorization flag protocol for the firm's top ten most complex clients, and a redesigned workpaper review process with documented judgment gates.

Scoring the intake automation: impact is medium-high — the admin currently spends roughly sixty hours per busy season on manual filing and the completeness failures cause an average of two to three mid-engagement interruptions per month. Risk is low — the system routes and flags, it does not make judgment calls, and an error means a document ends up in the wrong folder rather than producing a wrong client output. Readiness is high — the firm's email system is accessible, the client list is documented, and the admin can manage the transition in a week. Score: start here.

Scoring the Tier 2 flag protocol: impact is high — the firm's most complex clients generate the most liability exposure, and a flag protocol that surfaces capitalization and passive loss questions before review would change the quality of the sign-off meaningfully. Risk is medium — the flag logic has to be correct, and an incorrectly configured flag that misses a material issue is worse than no flag at all because it creates false confidence. Readiness is medium-low — the firm's client-specific rules are not documented, the categorization data for three clients is inconsistent, and neither senior practitioner has worked with a flag-based review process before. Score: build readiness first. Document the rules for the top five clients this quarter. Run a manual flag protocol for one engagement before automating it.

Scoring the workpaper review redesign: impact is high — the current review process is consuming senior time on mechanics that the AI already handled and skimming judgment sections that require the most attention. Risk is low — this is a process change, not a system deployment, and it does not introduce new failure modes. Readiness is medium — the redesign requires agreement between both senior practitioners on what the new review gates look like, which requires a structured conversation that has not happened yet. Score: start second, in parallel with intake automation, before the next busy season.

The sequence the matrix produces: intake automation in the next thirty days, workpaper review redesign over the next sixty days, Tier 2 flag protocol in the quarter after the rules are documented. Three initiatives, sequenced by what the firm can actually execute, with a clear readiness condition that has to be met before the highest-impact initiative begins. That is a plan a firm can commit to and measure.

What the Matrix Is Not

The matrix is not a guarantee. It identifies the best starting point given available information. That information will change as the first initiative is implemented and as the firm learns what it did not know before. The second initiative should be re-evaluated against the readiness conditions that actually exist at the time of implementation, not the ones that were estimated at the time of scoring. A prioritization matrix is a living document, not a locked plan.

The matrix is also not a substitute for a decision. A practitioner who uses the matrix to avoid committing to a starting point has misunderstood its purpose. The matrix produces a recommendation. Accepting or rejecting that recommendation is still a human judgment call — one that accounts for factors the matrix cannot score, including partner relationships, client expectations, and the firm's appetite for change at a particular moment. The matrix narrows the options. The practitioner makes the call.

Most importantly, the matrix is not the end of Part Two. It is the bridge to Part Three. The assessment identified the workflows. The matrix identified the sequence. What remains is how to execute — how to evaluate the systems that claim to do what you need, how to run a pilot without disrupting a tax season, how to price the recovered capacity, and how to build the kind of firm that compounds on each layer rather than replacing one manual process with a digital one and calling it transformation.

> *The matrix does not tell you what your firm will look like when you are done. It tells you what to do first. That is the only question that matters right now.*

Every firm that has built deliberately started with one initiative that worked. Not because it was the most ambitious. Because it was the right size for what the firm could execute, produced a result the team could see, and created the confidence and the institutional knowledge to attempt the next one. The prioritization matrix is how you find that initiative. The rest is execution.

THE MATRIX RULE	WHAT THIS IS NOT	THE BRIDGE
High impact + low risk + high readiness = start immediately. High impact + high risk + low readiness = **build readiness first, not the system.**	A locked plan. Re-score each initiative at implementation time against the readiness conditions that *actually exist* — not the ones estimated at scoring.	The assessment found the workflows. The matrix found the sequence. **Part Three is how to execute without disrupting a tax season.**

CHAPTER 9

The Right Questions

By the time you finish Part Two, you have something most firms never develop: a sequenced list of AI initiatives ranked by impact, risk, and readiness. You know what to build first. What you do not yet know is how to evaluate what you are being sold.

That distinction matters. The implementation playbook begins not with deployment but with evaluation — because the most common way firms waste the first twelve months of AI implementation is by choosing the wrong system before they understand what questions to ask about it.

The AI market for professional services is crowded and moving fast. Every vendor has a demo. Every demo is impressive. Every demo shows the system working on clean data, a favorable use case, and a problem the system was specifically designed to solve well. The demo is not a lie. It is a carefully constructed truth that tells you almost nothing about how the system will perform in your practice, on your clients' data, in the conditions you will actually encounter.

The demo shows you what the system can do. The right questions reveal what it will do — in your workflow, on your data, with your clients.

What follows is not a buyer's guide — the market will have changed by the time any specific recommendation ages well. It is a framework for evaluation that applies regardless of which system is on the other side of the table.

What You Are Actually Evaluating

Most practitioners evaluate AI systems on features. Can it handle the core workflow? Does it integrate with the systems already in use? Can it produce the deliverable in the format the engagement requires? These are threshold questions — if the answer is no, stop. But if the answer is yes, the feature evaluation has told you almost nothing useful. Every serious system in a given category can answer yes to the same threshold questions. The feature list is the floor, not the ceiling.

What actually differentiates systems is harder to see in a demo. It lives in the failure modes. What happens when the AI is wrong? What happens when the input data is messy? What happens when the classification is ambiguous? What happens when a client file has an edge case the system has never seen? A demo is designed to avoid every one of these questions. The right evaluation process forces them into the open.

Whose Judgment Is Encoded

Every AI system that makes a classification, a recommendation, or a flag is encoding judgment. The question is whose judgment, and whether it is the right judgment for your practice.

A general-purpose AI model has been trained on broad data. It knows the common patterns. It does not know that your client's situation has specific facts that change how those patterns apply. It does not know the judgment calls your practice has made consistently over years of work in a specific area. It does not know what you know. A transaction that looks routine to a general model may carry a consequence that only surfaces if the system understands the domain deeply enough to ask the right question about it.

Domain-specific systems are better, but the question remains: which domain, and built by whom? A system built by engineers with accounting consultants is different from a system built by CPAs who have spent years in the specific workflow the system is trying to automate. The former encodes a consultant's model of the workflow. The latter encodes a practitioner's model. The difference shows up in edge cases, in the flags the system surfaces, and in the quality of the output a CPA can actually sign.

The question to ask any vendor: what is the source of the domain logic in your system? Who encoded it, and what was their professional background? If the answer is "our model was trained on a large dataset of accounting transactions," the system is a Tier 1 automation. If the answer includes specific professional judgment rules — the logic that decides not just what category but what consequence — the system may be approaching Tier 2. The distinction is not marketing language. It is architecture.

> *The right question is not "does it categorize transactions." It is "what happens when the categorization has a material tax consequence and the system is uncertain."*

What Happens When It Is Wrong

Every AI system is wrong sometimes. The systems worth deploying in a professional context are not the ones that are never wrong — those do not exist. They are the ones that fail in ways a practitioner can catch, correct, and learn from.

There are two failure modes that matter. The first is visible failure: the system flags its uncertainty, escalates the item for review, and makes the problem clear. This is the correct failure mode for professional services AI. The second is invisible failure: the system produces a confident output that is wrong, and the error is not visible unless you already know the right answer. The first failure mode makes you more effective. The second makes you liable for something you did not catch.

The way to test failure behavior is not to ask the vendor about their accuracy rate. Accuracy rates are measured on test data. Your clients' files are not test data. The way to test failure behavior is to run a deliberately messy file through the system during evaluation — a file with mixed personal and business expenses, an entity structure the system has not seen before, a transaction description that is genuinely ambiguous. Watch what the system does with it. Does it produce a confident wrong answer, or does it surface the item for judgment? The answer tells you more than any accuracy statistic.

A related question: what is the override mechanism? A system that allows a CPA to override a classification, record why, and have that correction inform future outputs is building institutional memory. A system that allows overrides but does not learn from them is a static tool. A system that does not allow overrides at all is not suitable for professional services use — it removes the judgment layer that makes the output defensible.

Where Does It Run, and Who Owns the Output

The data architecture question is the one most practitioners skip in vendor evaluations, and the one that generates the most problems after deployment. There are three sub-questions that matter.

First: where does client data go when it enters the system? Cloud-based AI systems that process client financial data are subject to the same professional obligations as any other service provider. Professional confidentiality rules govern how client information can be disclosed and to whom. For tax practitioners, IRC §216 governs the use of tax return information specifically. For auditors and controllers, engagement agreements and professional standards set the boundary. Before deploying any AI system on client data, you need a clear answer to the question: whose servers does this data touch, what are their data handling obligations, and what does the agreement say about data use? "Enterprise-grade security" is not an answer to this question. A data processing agreement is.

The infrastructure landscape is moving toward local execution — AI systems that run on the firm's own hardware, with data that never leaves the firm's environment. This architecture addresses the confidentiality question directly. It is not yet widely available for most AI professional services systems, but it is coming, and it will become a competitive differentiator for practices serving institutional or high-net-worth clients with strict data governance requirements. When evaluating systems, ask whether a private deployment option exists or is on the roadmap.

Second: is client data siloed? A system that improves its classifications by learning across all client data in the platform is training on your clients' confidential information to benefit other users. This is a different question from whether data is secure. Data can be secure and still be used in ways that create professional responsibility problems. The question to ask explicitly: does data from one client's account influence outputs for another client's account? If yes, understand exactly how before proceeding.

Third: who owns the output? A workpaper generated by an AI system and reviewed and approved by a CPA is the CPA's work product. The professional liability attaches to the signature, not to the system that assisted in its preparation. But vendor agreements vary, and some contain language about ownership of outputs, derivative works, or the right to use anonymized outputs for model improvement. Read the agreement. The output you sign is yours. Make sure the agreement treats it that way.

Where the System Stops and You Begin

The most important architectural feature of any AI system deployed in a professional services context is its judgment boundary — the explicit line between what the system decides and what the CPA decides. Every serious system has one. The question is whether it is designed deliberately or incidentally.

A system with a deliberate judgment boundary surfaces items that require professional review, presents them with enough context to make the review meaningful, and records the reviewer's decision and reasoning. The CPA is not reviewing to rubber-stamp — the CPA is reviewing because the system recognized that professional judgment is required at that point in the workflow. The system does the production. The CPA does the judgment. The signature goes on the output. The liability stays where it belongs.

A system without a deliberate judgment boundary either asks for your review on everything — which eliminates the efficiency benefit — or routes items to review inconsistently, creating the risk that material issues are presented as routine items and treated accordingly. Neither failure mode is obvious in a demo. Both are visible within the first engagement cycle after deployment.

The question to ask in every vendor conversation: show me what a flagged item looks like. Show me the review interface. Show me what the system asks the CPA to decide, and what information it provides to support that decision. If the vendor cannot demonstrate the review interface specifically, the judgment boundary is an afterthought. If they can demonstrate it clearly, and if it provides enough context to make a genuine professional judgment rather than a mechanical approval, the system was designed for the right kind of CPA relationship.

> *AI suggests. The professional decides. That sentence should describe the architecture, not just the marketing copy.*

Build vs. Buy: When to Encode Your Own Logic

The build-versus-buy decision is the one most practitioners reach too quickly in one direction or the other. Practitioners who have never built software assume buying is the only option. Practitioners who have experimented with AI coding environments sometimes overcorrect in the other direction, building systems that encode their logic in ways that are fragile, undocumented, and difficult to maintain.

The right decision depends on one question: does a system exist that encodes the specific domain logic your practice requires, fails visibly rather than silently, handles your data responsibly, and maintains a clear line between what the system decides and what you decide? If yes, buy it. The competitive advantage is not in building the software — it is in deploying it well and earlier than the competition.

If no such system exists, the build decision becomes more interesting. The firms that have built their own AI workflow systems are not doing it because building is better than buying. They are doing it because the workflow they need to automate is specific enough, and the domain logic specific enough, that no commercial system has encoded it correctly. A practice with fifteen years of deep work in a specific area has classification rules, flag logic, and review standards that are not available in any commercial system. Building a system that encodes those rules is not a technology project. It is a practice-differentiation project.

The cost of building has dropped substantially. The availability of AI-assisted development environments means that if you have domain expertise and a willingness to engage with the build process, you can now create systems that would have required a dedicated engineering team five years ago. The bottleneck has shifted from the cost of building to the quality of the domain logic being encoded. A poorly designed system built quickly is not an advantage. A well-designed system that encodes years of professional judgment is a moat.

The practical guidance: buy before you build. Evaluate what exists. If a commercial system answers the right questions — whose logic is encoded, how it fails, where the data goes, and where your judgment begins — deploy it. If it does not, the build decision deserves a serious evaluation. Not as a technology adventure, but as a deliberate practice investment with a clear articulation of what domain logic you are encoding and why it produces better outcomes for your clients.

The Readiness Check Before Deployment

The prioritization matrix in Chapter 8 included a readiness dimension for a reason. Buying a system before the workflow is ready to support it is one of the most common and most expensive mistakes in AI implementation. The system is not the problem. The workflow is.

Before deploying any AI system on live client work, three readiness conditions should be confirmed. The first is data readiness. The AI system will only perform as well as the data it receives. If client documents arrive inconsistently, if transaction descriptions are idiosyncratic, if the chart of accounts varies by client without documented logic, the system will produce inconsistent outputs — not because the system is poor but because the inputs are. Cleaning up the data intake process is not preparation for AI deployment. It is a prerequisite for it.

The second is workflow readiness. Your review process needs to be designed for AI output before AI output starts flowing through it. A review workflow designed for manually prepared workpapers will not translate directly to reviewing AI-assisted output. The judgment gates are in different places. The things that require human attention are different. If you adopt an AI system without redesigning the review workflow, you will spend the first season reviewing AI output the same way you reviewed manually prepared output — which means inspecting everything instead of directing attention to the items that require professional judgment. The efficiency gain disappears.

The third is staff readiness. AI systems change what people do, not just how fast they do it. Staff who have been doing production work — transaction coding, workpaper preparation, document organization — will need to shift toward reviewing AI output, resolving flags, and escalating genuine judgment questions. This is a different skill set and, for many practitioners, a more demanding one. A staff member who reviews AI output without understanding the logic behind the flag is not adding the judgment layer the system was designed to require. Training before deployment is not optional. It is the difference between a system that elevates the practice and one that just adds a new interface to the existing workload.

The Vendor Conversation, Done Right

Armed with the right questions and the three readiness conditions, the vendor conversation looks different from a typical software evaluation. The vendor is not presenting to someone who is impressed by the demo and looking for reasons to buy. They are presenting to you — someone who already knows what you need, and is determining whether this system provides it.

The questions that matter: Who encoded the domain logic in this system, and what is their professional background in this workflow? Show me how the system handles an item it is uncertain about — not a clean file, a messy one. Where does client data go, and what does your data processing agreement say about how it is used? Show me the review interface for a flagged item. What does the CPA actually see, and what are they being asked to decide? Does a private deployment option exist for practices with strict data governance requirements?

A vendor who cannot answer these questions clearly is selling a demo, not a system. A vendor who answers them well, whose architecture reflects the same understanding of professional services AI that this chapter has described, is worth the next conversation. The evaluation is not complete — that requires running the system on real client data in a controlled pilot, which is the subject of Chapter 10. But the vendor conversation, done with the right questions, will eliminate most of the wrong choices before the pilot ever begins.

The practitioners who will build AI-ready firms are not the ones who buy the most systems or move the fastest. They are the ones who choose deliberately, deploy on a workflow that is ready for it, and maintain the judgment layer that makes every output they sign defensible. The right questions are how that process starts.

> *The bottleneck has shifted. It is no longer access to AI. It is the quality of the domain logic you have encoded — and the discipline to ask the right questions before you deploy it.*

CHAPTER 10

Running the Pilot

The evaluation is complete. You have identified a system that encodes the right logic, fails visibly, handles your data responsibly, and maintains a clear line between what it decides and what you decide. You know which workflow you are deploying it on first. The prioritization matrix told you that. What comes next is not deployment. It is a pilot — and the distinction matters more than most practitioners expect.

A pilot is not a test of whether the system works. The evaluation already established that. A pilot is a test of whether the system works in your practice, on your clients' work, with your staff running it, under the actual conditions of your busiest time of year. Those conditions are different from every demo environment, every reference client the vendor showed you, and every use case in the documentation. The pilot is where the gap between the system's design and your practice's reality becomes visible.

Most pilots fail not because the system is wrong but because the pilot is designed wrong. The scope is too broad. The timing is too aggressive. The success criteria are undefined. The staff running it were not prepared for what AI-assisted review actually feels like in practice. The result is a chaotic first cycle that produces no useful signal and leaves the firm more skeptical of AI implementation than it was before it started.

> *A pilot designed wrong does not tell you whether the system works. It tells you whether the pilot worked. Those are different questions.*

This chapter is about designing the pilot right — scoping it correctly, timing it deliberately, defining what success looks like before the first engagement runs through it, and extracting the signal that determines whether to expand, adjust, or stop.

Scope: One Workflow, One Segment, One Cycle

The most common pilot mistake is scope creep before the first cycle is complete. A firm decides to pilot an AI system on client intake, and by the second week has also started running transaction classification and workpaper preparation through it. Each addition feels logical — the system can handle it, the workflow is adjacent, the efficiency gain seems obvious. By the end of the first cycle, three workflows have been partially automated, none has been properly evaluated, and the firm cannot tell which changes produced which results.

The right scope for a pilot is the smallest unit that produces a complete, evaluable result. One workflow. One segment of your client base. One full engagement cycle. That constraint feels limiting when the system could theoretically do more. It is not limiting — it is the only way to get clean signal.

Choosing the right client segment for the pilot matters as much as choosing the right workflow. The pilot clients should be representative of the workflow you are automating, but they should not be your most complex or your most sensitive. Highly complex engagements introduce too many variables. Highly sensitive client relationships introduce too much risk if something goes wrong. The right pilot segment is the clients whose work is typical enough to generate representative signal and whose relationship is strong enough to survive a correction if the system produces something unexpected.

A practical starting size: five to ten engagements for the first pilot cycle. Enough to generate a pattern. Small enough to monitor closely. Large enough that one outlier does not distort the result.

Timing: Before Busy Season, Not During It

The timing of a pilot is the second most common failure point. Firms frequently launch AI pilots during busy season — partly because that is when the pain of manual workflows is most acute, and partly because it feels like the right time to prove that the system can handle real volume under real pressure. Both of those instincts are wrong.

Busy season is the worst time to introduce a new system into the workflow. Staff capacity is at its lowest. Error tolerance is at its lowest. The cost of a problem — a misclassification, a review queue that does not surface a material item, a staff member who does not know how to resolve a flag — is at its highest. A pilot launched during busy season is not a pilot. It is a stress test of an untrained system on your most critical work. The results will be bad, and they will be bad for reasons that have nothing to do with whether the system is capable.

The right timing is the cycle immediately before your next busy season. That window gives you enough time to run a complete pilot on real engagements, evaluate the results, retrain staff on what you learned, adjust the workflow, and enter busy season with a system that has already been through one cycle of real work. The pilot is preparation. Busy season is deployment.

> *You do not want to learn what the system cannot do during your busiest month. You want to know that before it starts.*

If the pre-season window has already passed and you are evaluating this during or approaching a busy period, the right answer is to wait. Schedule the pilot for the next available off-peak window. The system will still be there. The cost of a poorly timed pilot — to client relationships, to staff confidence, to the firm's appetite for AI implementation — is higher than the cost of waiting one cycle.

Define Success Before the First Engagement Runs

The most important preparation step for a pilot is one that most firms skip entirely: defining what success looks like before the pilot begins. Without a definition of success established in advance, the evaluation at the end of the pilot becomes a subjective conversation shaped by whoever had the most frustrating experience. The practitioner who had three flag escalations in a row decides the system is unreliable. The staff member who found the review interface confusing decides the system is not ready. The partner who reviewed the output without knowing what to expect decides it needs more work. None of those observations is wrong. None of them is sufficient to make a deployment decision.

Success criteria for a pilot should be specific, measurable, and established before the first engagement runs through the system. The criteria do not need to be sophisticated. They need to be agreed upon. Some examples of criteria that produce useful signal: the system correctly classifies a defined percentage of routine items without manual intervention; flagged items are resolved by the reviewer using the information the system provides, without requiring outside research to make the decision; the total review time for a pilot engagement is less than the baseline review time for the same engagement in the prior cycle; no material items are missed — every item that required professional judgment was surfaced for review.

The last criterion is the most important one. Accuracy on routine items is a Tier 1 metric. It tells you the system is processing correctly. The metric that matters for professional services is whether the judgment layer functions — whether the system reliably surfaces the items that require your attention. A system that classifies routine items with high accuracy but occasionally routes a material judgment question as a routine item is not a system you can rely on. The pilot is the only way to test this on your work.

Preparing Your Staff for What AI-Assisted Review Actually Feels Like

Staff preparation is the most frequently underestimated part of a pilot. Practitioners who have spent years doing production work — building workpapers from scratch, organizing source documents, coding transactions manually — experience AI-assisted workflows differently than they expect. The production layer disappears. What remains is a review queue of flags, escalations, and judgment calls. That is a different kind of work, and for many people it feels more demanding, not less, at least initially.

The discomfort is real and worth acknowledging before the pilot starts. When a staff member has spent years doing a task manually, the sudden removal of that task creates uncertainty about their role. The flag queue that replaces it requires them to make judgment calls they previously deferred. The system's confidence in its own outputs can feel like pressure to approve without scrutiny. None of these dynamics are problems with the system. They are normal responses to a workflow change that requires a different kind of attention.

Before the pilot begins, walk your staff through three things. First, what the system does and does not do — specifically, what the judgment boundary is and why items appear in the review queue. Second, what a good review looks like — not approving everything the system produces, but genuinely evaluating each flagged item against the context provided. Third, how to escalate — what to do when a flag does not provide enough information to make a decision, and who to bring in when the judgment call requires more experience than the reviewer has.

The goal of staff preparation is not to make the pilot go smoothly. It is to make the feedback useful. A staff member who understands the system and still finds a flaw in the review interface is giving you signal. A staff member who was never prepared and found the whole experience confusing is giving you noise.

Running the Pilot: What to Watch

Once the pilot is running, your job is observation, not optimization. The most common mistake during a live pilot is making adjustments in real time — changing the review workflow, adjusting the classification rules, retraining staff on the fly. Each change introduces a new variable that makes the final evaluation harder to interpret. Unless you encounter a critical failure that threatens client work, hold the workflow steady for the full pilot cycle. The point is to learn how the system performs under your actual conditions, not how it performs after you have compensated for its weaknesses.

There are four things worth tracking actively during the pilot. First, flag volume and type. How many items per engagement are being surfaced for review? Are the flags concentrated in specific transaction types, client categories, or workflow stages? High flag volume is not necessarily a problem — it may reflect a workflow that has more judgment-intensive work than you realized. Consistently low flag volume on complex engagements is a warning sign.

Second, reviewer resolution rate. Are reviewers resolving flags using the information the system provides, or are they frequently going outside the system to find the context they need? High outside-research rates indicate the system's judgment boundary is not providing enough context to make the decision the system is asking for.

Third, override patterns. When reviewers override the system's classification or recommendation, what are the common reasons? Random overrides indicate inconsistent reviewer judgment. Systematic overrides — the same type of item being corrected repeatedly — indicate a gap in the system's domain logic that needs to be addressed before full deployment.

Fourth, time to complete. Track how long each pilot engagement takes from start to signed output, and compare it to the baseline for similar engagements in prior cycles. Do not expect a dramatic time reduction in the first pilot cycle. Staff are learning the system. The workflow is new. The signal you are looking for is directional — is the time moving in the right direction, and for which parts of the engagement?

Reading the Results: Expand, Adjust, or Stop

At the end of the pilot cycle, you have three options: expand to full deployment, adjust and run another pilot cycle, or stop. Each outcome is legitimate. The pilot is designed to produce one of these three results, not necessarily the first one.

Expand when the success criteria are met, the override patterns are explainable and addressable, the staff feedback is substantive rather than resistant, and no material items were missed during the cycle. Expansion does not mean deploying across the entire practice immediately. It means moving to the next segment of the client base while the current segment continues at full deployment. Controlled expansion is how you build confidence without creating catastrophic failure modes.

Adjust when the success criteria were partially met, the override patterns reveal a specific and addressable gap, and the staff feedback identifies a clear workflow problem rather than a system problem. An adjustment cycle is not a failure — it is the pilot working correctly. The gap between the system's design and your practice's reality was identified before busy season rather than during it. Fix the specific issue, run another cycle on the same scope, and evaluate again.

Stop when the success criteria were not met, the override patterns indicate a fundamental gap in the system's domain logic that the vendor cannot address, or a material item was missed during the cycle and the review process did not catch it before sign-off. Stopping a pilot is not a failure of AI implementation. It is a correct application of the evaluation process. A system that fails a well-designed pilot would have failed in production, at greater cost and with greater consequences.

> *The pilot that tells you to stop is not a failed pilot. It is the pilot doing exactly what it was designed to do.*

What a Successful Pilot Produces

A pilot that meets its success criteria produces more than a deployment decision. It produces institutional knowledge that no vendor demo, no reference client, and no documentation can provide: the specific knowledge of how this system performs on your work, with your clients, under your conditions.

That knowledge is the foundation of everything that follows in the implementation playbook. You know which flag types your reviewers resolve quickly and which ones require escalation. You know which client segments generate the most override activity. You know which parts of the workflow the system handles reliably and which parts still require manual intervention. You know what your staff can do with this system and what they need more training on before you expand.

You also know something more valuable than any of that: the system works in your practice. Not in a demo. Not at a reference client. In your practice, on your clients' work, with your team. That is the only proof that matters when you are deciding whether to build the rest of your practice around it.

Chapter 11 addresses what happens next — how to convert a successful pilot into a practice-wide deployment, how to price the recovered capacity rather than give it away, and how to build the kind of firm that compounds on each layer of AI implementation rather than treating each one as a standalone efficiency project.

Pricing the Efficiency Gains

The pilot is complete. The system works. You have recovered capacity — hours that used to go to production work that the AI now handles. The question that follows is the one most practices get wrong: what do you do with those hours?

The instinctive answer is to pass the savings to clients. Fees come down. The engagement takes less time, so it costs less. The client is happy. The practice looks efficient. This is the answer that turns AI implementation from a competitive advantage into a commodity race — and it is happening at scale across professional services right now. Clients at the largest firms in the world are demanding fee reductions because AI compressed work that previously took forty hours into something that takes a fraction of that. When a client can quantify how much time AI saved you, they will ask for a share of it. And they will get it, if you have not already repriced the work on your own terms.

Recovered capacity passed to clients as lower fees is not a pricing strategy. It is a subsidy. You are funding your client's cost reduction with your own margin.

The practices that capture the value of AI implementation are the ones that reprice deliberately — not by raising fees arbitrarily, but by shifting what the fee covers. The production is no longer what you are selling. The judgment is. And judgment at scale — applied to more clients, more complex situations, with more depth than was previously possible — is worth more, not less, than the production it replaced.

The Hourly Model's Structural Problem

The hourly billing model has a structural problem that AI makes impossible to ignore. It prices professional services by the cost of production, not the value of the output. An engagement that takes twenty hours billed at a standard rate produces the same revenue as an engagement that takes twenty hours on a more complex matter, even though the value delivered — the judgment applied, the risk identified, the consequence avoided — is entirely different.

When production was the bottleneck, this structural problem was invisible. The hours required to produce a deliverable were roughly correlated with its complexity, because complex work took more time. AI breaks that correlation. A deliverable that previously required twelve hours of production work may now require two hours of AI-assisted production and one hour of professional review. The value of that deliverable — the judgment behind it, the liability it carries, the signature that makes it defensible — has not changed. But the hourly model prices it as if it has.

The practices that are already feeling this pressure are the ones billing clients who have noticed. Clients who have read about AI efficiency gains ask why a deliverable that took eight hours last year is taking eight hours this year. The honest answer — that the eight hours now includes more judgment and less production than it did previously — is not a conversation the hourly model is designed to have. The hourly model says: this work cost eight hours. It does not say: this work required thirty years of domain expertise applied to a question that could have cost you significantly more if it were answered incorrectly.

What You Are Actually Selling

The repricing conversation begins with clarity about what the engagement actually delivers. Not what it costs to produce. What it delivers.

For most professional services engagements, what is being delivered is a defensible output — a signed deliverable that the client can present to a lender, a regulator, an auditor, or a counterparty, with confidence that a licensed professional has reviewed it and stands behind it. The production that precedes the signature is not the product. The signature is the product. The judgment behind the signature is what makes it worth paying for.

When you frame the engagement this way, the repricing argument becomes straightforward. AI compressed the production. The judgment layer — the review, the professional oversight, the liability that attaches to the signature — did not change. What changed is that you can now apply that judgment layer to more clients, in more depth, with more consistency than was previously possible. That is not a cost reduction. That is a capacity expansion at the judgment layer. The right pricing response is to charge for the judgment, not the hours.

> *The signature is the product.*
> *Price it accordingly.*

Three Ways to Reprice Recovered Capacity

There is no single right pricing model for every practice. The right approach depends on your client mix, your existing fee structure, and how much of your capacity AI has actually recovered. What follows are three approaches that work in different contexts. Most practices will use some combination of all three over time.

The first is fixed-fee repricing. If you have been billing an engagement by the hour and AI has materially reduced the hours required, the correct response is not to reduce the fee proportionally. It is to convert the engagement to a fixed fee priced at the value of the output. The client gets certainty — they know what the engagement costs before it begins. You get margin protection — the fee is no longer exposed to client inquiries about hours. The engagement is now priced on what it delivers, not what it costs you to produce.

Fixed-fee repricing works best for engagements with predictable scope and a well-defined deliverable. The pilot gave you the data you need to price it: you know how long the AI-assisted workflow takes, you know where the judgment-intensive steps are, and you know the variability in the work. Price the fixed fee at a level that reflects the value of the output and provides enough margin to absorb the occasional complex engagement that runs over.

The second is capacity redeployment. Rather than reducing fees, you use the recovered capacity to serve more clients at the same fee level. If AI has reduced the production time per engagement by forty percent, you can serve forty percent more clients with the same team. That is revenue growth without headcount growth — the most direct path from AI implementation to practice profitability.

Capacity redeployment requires that you have demand waiting. If your practice is currently turning away clients or managing a waitlist, this is the highest-value use of recovered capacity. If your practice is at capacity and not turning anyone away, the recovered capacity is the raw material for business development — the hours that used to go to production are now available for the conversations, the relationships, and the visibility that attract new clients.

The third is service expansion. Recovered production capacity creates room for advisory work that previously could not fit in the engagement timeline. The client whose deliverable used to consume twelve hours of production now gets that same deliverable plus a conversation about what it means, what the risks are, and what they should consider doing differently. That conversation is Tier 3 work — proactive advisory that surfaces the question before the client thinks to ask it. It is also work that commands a premium because it is not available from practices that are still spending all their capacity on production.

Having the Repricing Conversation with Existing Clients

The hardest part of repricing is not the math. It is the conversation with existing clients who have been paying hourly fees and now expect those fees to come down. That conversation is easier when you have a clear framework for it — and harder when you are trying to improvise one on the spot.

The framework that works is straightforward: you are changing what you are selling, not how much you are charging. Previously, the fee covered the hours required to produce the deliverable. Going forward, the fee covers the deliverable itself — the review, the judgment, the liability, and the professional standing behind the output. The production cost has changed. The value of the output has not. You are converting to a pricing model that reflects the latter rather than the former.

Most clients understand this framing when it is presented clearly. What they resist is the version of this conversation where the practice is obviously capturing efficiency gains without offering anything in return. The repricing conversation goes better when it is paired with something — the fixed fee that gives the client cost certainty, the advisory conversation that did not fit in the engagement before, the faster turnaround that the AI-assisted workflow makes possible. The client is not being asked to pay the same for less. They are being asked to pay for a defined output rather than an undefined number of hours.

For clients who push back, the honest response is this: the alternative to fixed-fee pricing is hourly pricing that will produce a lower number as AI continues to compress production time. A fixed fee that reflects the value of the output protects both parties — the client from the uncertainty of variable hours, and the practice from the pressure to reduce fees as production costs continue to fall. That is a conversation worth having directly.

Pricing New Clients Correctly from the Start

New clients are easier. They have no baseline to compare against. They do not know what the engagement used to cost when it was entirely manual. They are evaluating the fee against the value of the output and the alternatives available to them — which is exactly the comparison you want them making.

Price new engagements on a fixed-fee or value-based model from the first conversation. Do not introduce an hourly structure that you will need to reprice later. The engagement should have a defined scope and a defined fee that reflects the value of the deliverable. If the scope changes, the fee changes — not because hours changed, but because the deliverable changed.

New clients acquired after AI implementation are also a signal about market positioning. If you are attracting clients who chose your practice over alternatives, the reason is rarely the fee. It is the credibility, the responsiveness, the quality of the output, and the depth of the advisory relationship. Those are the things AI enables when the recovered capacity is deployed correctly. They are also the things that justify fees above the market rate for practices that are still selling production hours.

The Margin Structure of an AI-Ready Practice

When the repricing is done correctly — fixed fees on core engagements, recovered capacity redeployed to advisory or new clients, new clients priced on value rather than hours — the margin structure of the practice changes in a way that compounds over time.

The first cycle of AI implementation reduces production costs per engagement. The repricing captures that as margin rather than passing it to clients. The recovered capacity generates additional revenue through more clients or higher-value advisory work. The second cycle of AI implementation — as the system learns from the corrections and flags generated during the first cycle — reduces production costs further. The margin that was captured in the first cycle is now the foundation for investing in the second.

This is the compounding structure that separates the practices that build durable advantage from the ones that implement AI and hand the savings to clients. The difference is not the AI system. It is the pricing decision made after the first successful pilot.

Practices that price correctly after AI implementation end up with a margin structure that looks more like a software company than a traditional professional services firm. Fixed costs are relatively stable. Revenue per client grows as the advisory layer expands. The constraint is no longer hours — it is the number of client relationships the judgment layer can support. That is a fundamentally different business than one that grows by hiring more people to do more hours of production work.

> *The firms that implement AI and keep hourly pricing are working harder for the same revenue. The firms that reprice correctly are building a different kind of practice entirely.*

Chapter 12 addresses what that different kind of practice looks like — not as an aspiration, but as a concrete description of the firm that built deliberately, layer by layer, and what distinguishes it from the firm that watched from the sidelines.

What the Firm Looks Like in Three Years

Three years is the right horizon for this conversation. One year is too short — AI implementation compounds slowly at first and most of the visible change happens in years two and three. Five years is too long — the technology is moving fast enough that specific predictions become unreliable past the near term. Three years is where the choices made today become visible as outcomes.

What follows are two portraits. They describe practices that started from the same place — similar size, similar client base, similar team, similar awareness that AI was changing the profession. The difference between them is not talent, not resources, and not luck. It is a sequence of decisions: whether to move deliberately or wait, and what to do with the results of each decision.

Neither portrait is hypothetical. Both are composites of patterns that are already visible across professional services practices that moved early and those that did not. The details are not predictions. They are extrapolations of trajectories that are already in motion.

The Firm That Built Deliberately

Three years ago, this practice looked like most others. The team was good. The clients were loyal. The work was done manually, mostly on schedule, mostly without errors. The pressure to change was present but not yet acute — AI was something other firms were experimenting with, something worth watching.

What happened next was not dramatic. It was a sequence of small decisions, each one enabled by the one before it. The first decision was to audit one workflow — not the whole practice, one workflow — and understand exactly where the production was and where the judgment was. The second decision was to pilot an AI system on that workflow, on a small segment of clients, before busy season. The third decision was to reprice the recovered capacity rather than pass it to clients.

None of those decisions felt transformational at the time. The first pilot covered eight clients. The time savings were real but modest. The repricing conversation was awkward with two clients and straightforward with the rest. By the end of the first year, the practice had one AI-assisted workflow running well, a fee structure that reflected the value of the output rather than the cost of the production, and a team that understood how to review AI output rather than produce it.

The second year looked different. The first workflow was stable enough to run without active management. The recovered capacity from year one was available for the second workflow. The team had internalized the review discipline from year one and applied it faster to year two. The compounding had begun — not at a dramatic rate, but at a rate that was clearly accelerating.

By year three, this practice looks recognizably different from where it started. The differences are not visible in the signage or the website. They are visible in the numbers, in the client relationships, and in what the team spends its time on.

Revenue per client is higher. Not because fees were raised arbitrarily, but because the advisory layer that AI made possible is valued by clients who now receive it. The clients who were not interested in advisory work have been gently redirected toward practices better suited to transaction-only relationships. The clients who remained deepened their engagement.

Client capacity is higher. The same team serves meaningfully more clients than it did three years ago. The production constraint has been largely removed. The new constraint is the judgment layer — the number of client relationships that can receive genuine professional attention. That is a constraint worth having, because it is the constraint that commands a premium.

The team works differently. The junior staff are not coding transactions or building workpapers from scratch. They are reviewing AI output, resolving flags, escalating judgment questions, and learning the domain logic that makes those judgment calls correct. They are developing expertise faster than the previous generation of staff, because the production work that used to occupy most of their time has been removed and replaced with work that requires and develops judgment. The pipeline of capable senior practitioners is better than it was three years ago, not worse.

New clients are different too. The practice has a reputation for responsiveness, for output quality, and for the depth of advisory thinking that comes with engagements. It attracts clients who are looking for that, and turns away clients who are looking primarily for the lowest fee. That self-selection has improved the average quality and complexity of the work, which has further developed the team's capabilities, which has further improved the quality of the advisory layer. The flywheel is running.

> *The practice does not look like a technology company. It looks like a professional services firm that is unusually good at what it does, unusually responsive, and unusually profitable for its size.*

The Firm That Waited

Three years ago, this practice also looked like most others. Same starting point. Good team, loyal clients, manual workflows, awareness that AI was worth watching. The difference is what happened next.

The waiting was not passive. It was active waiting — the kind that feels like prudence. Subscriptions to AI tools were purchased and evaluated. Staff attended conferences where AI was discussed. The practice leadership read articles, watched demos, and concluded that the technology was not yet ready for their specific workflows, or that their clients were not yet asking for it, or that the risk of implementation during busy season was too high to justify moving forward now.

Each year, the same conversation happened. The technology had moved forward. New systems were available. The case for moving was stronger. And each year, the same conclusion: not yet. The timing was not right. The right system had not been found. The team needed more preparation. There was always a reason to wait one more cycle.

By year three, the waiting has produced its own consequences. They are not catastrophic — the practice is still operating, still serving clients, still billing work. But the trajectory has changed in ways that are now difficult to reverse.

Fee pressure has arrived. Not from a single client conversation but from a pattern — clients who have read about AI efficiency asking why costs are not coming down, clients comparing the practice's fees to alternatives that have moved, clients who do not renew engagements without a conversation about pricing that was not necessary two years ago. The hourly model that felt stable is no longer self-evident to clients who have become aware of what AI can do to production costs.

Talent is harder. The staff members who were most interested in AI implementation left — not necessarily to competitors, but to practices and roles where the work was more interesting and the trajectory was clearer. The staff who remained are good at manual workflows. They have not developed the review discipline and judgment skills that come from working alongside AI systems for two years. Recruiting new staff who have those skills requires paying for them, and the margin structure of the practice does not yet support the premium.

New client acquisition is harder. The practices that moved early have reputations and referral networks that reflect their capabilities. The practice that waited is competing for clients who have not yet heard about the difference — a shrinking pool as more clients become sophisticated about what AI-ready professional services looks like.

Implementation is now more expensive. The systems have improved, but the gap between this practice's current state and what is required to deploy them well has widened. The workflows are still manual. The data is still inconsistent. The team has not developed review discipline. A practice that could have piloted one workflow three years ago with eight clients and modest disruption now faces a more complex, more expensive, more disruptive implementation with less margin to absorb the transition cost.

> *The waiting did not reduce the risk of implementation. It increased the cost of it.*

The Gap Is Not Closing

The most important thing to understand about the gap between these two practices is that it is not closing. It is widening. The practice that built deliberately has two years of institutional knowledge, a trained team, a stable AI-assisted workflow, and a compounding margin structure. The practice that waited has none of those things and is now trying to build them under more pressure, with less time, and at higher cost.

AICPA research published in early 2026 found that only 26 percent of firms had made the transition to what it described as AI-transformed operations — and that the gap between that group and the rest was widening, not closing. The firms pulling ahead were not doing so because they had better AI systems. They were doing so because they had made decisions earlier, learned from them, and built on what they learned. The advantage is not the technology. It is the institutional knowledge that comes from having used the technology under real conditions.

That institutional knowledge cannot be purchased. It cannot be imported. It can only be built, engagement by engagement, cycle by cycle, correction by correction. A practice that has two years of it cannot be caught by a practice that is starting today, not in the near term. The gap is structural.

The Decision Is Still Available

If you have read this far without having started, the portrait of the practice that waited may feel like a description of where you are heading. That is intentional. It is also not a verdict.

The decision to move deliberately is still available today. The window has not closed. What has changed is the cost of the delay already incurred — the institutional knowledge that was not built, the margin that was not captured, the staff who did not develop review discipline during two years of AI-assisted work. Those costs are real. They are also finite. The practice that starts today is not starting from the same place as the practice that started three years ago, but it is still starting from a place where the decision matters.

The urgency is not manufactured. The AICPA data, the shifts at large firms, the fee pressure that is arriving in client conversations across the profession — these are not predictions. They are current conditions. The practices that respond to them now will be in a different position in three years than the practices that respond in two years. Both will be in a better position than the practices that do not respond at all.

The implementation playbook in Part Three was designed for a practice that is ready to move. Chapter 9 gave you the questions to ask. Chapter 10 gave you a pilot design that does not require betting the practice on the first cycle. Chapter 11 gave you the pricing logic that converts recovered capacity into margin rather than discounts. This chapter gives you the destination.

The next chapter is the last one. It does not give you more steps. It gives you the frame — what the profession is becoming, what survives the transition, and what the practice that built deliberately is positioned to do in a world where the production layer has largely disappeared.

What Survives

The profession is not disappearing. The shape of it is changing in ways that are now moving faster than most practitioners expected, and the change is not distributed evenly. Some practices will emerge from this transition more capable, more valuable, and more profitable than they have ever been. Others will find that the work they built their practice around has been repriced, commoditized, or automated away — and that the window to reposition closed while they were deciding whether to move.

This book has been about how to be in the first group. The framework, the workflow assessment, the implementation playbook — all of it is in service of a single outcome: a practice that is positioned on the right side of what is about to become a permanent and widening gap.

This final chapter is not another step. It is the view from the end of the road — what the profession looks like from here, what gets compressed and what gets elevated, and what the practices that survive will have in common.

The Hourglass

Think of the profession as an hourglass. The wide part at the top is the work that requires genuine professional judgment — the advisory conversation, the interpretation of ambiguous facts, the recommendation that depends on understanding a client's specific situation rather than applying a general rule. The wide part at the bottom is the production work — the data entry, the reconciliation, the document organization, the mechanical preparation of deliverables. The narrow middle is the supervision of production work that requires some professional knowledge but not genuine judgment.

For most of the profession's history, the hourglass was filled from the bottom. Production work was where young professionals spent most of their time, because production work was how the knowledge necessary for judgment was accumulated. You learned how to interpret a complex situation by first spending years preparing the documentation of complex situations. The narrow middle was where most practitioners spent most of their careers. The wide top was reserved for the most senior, and only for the most demanding engagements.

AI is collapsing the middle and the bottom. The production layer — the data entry, the reconciliation, the mechanical preparation — is already largely automatable at Tier 1. The narrow middle — the supervision of production work that requires professional knowledge to oversee — is being compressed by Tier 2 systems that encode that oversight logic and apply it consistently without a human supervisor in the loop for every item. What remains, and what cannot be automated, is the wide part at the top: the judgment, the interpretation, the relationship, the accountability.

> *An AI cannot sign. Everything that follows from that sentence is what this book has been about.*

The hourglass is not a threat to the profession. It is a restructuring of it. The practitioners who survive — and who thrive — are not the ones who resist the compression of the middle. They are the ones who move to the top before the compression reaches them, and who position their practices to do the work that only the credential, the judgment, and the liability can anchor.

What Is Already Happening

The hourglass is not a prediction. It is a description of a process already visible in the data and in the decisions being made at the largest firms in the profession.

PwC has announced a shift of significant portions of its tax and consulting services toward AI-powered automated delivery — subscription-based, without a PwC professional in the loop for every output. The explicit goal is a model where the firm's accumulated expertise is encoded into systems that clients access directly. That is Tier 2 intelligence delivered at Tier 1 cost. The human judgment layer is reserved for the engagements where the client relationship, the complexity, or the liability requires it.

The fee pressure that follows from this is already visible. When KPMG demanded fee reductions from a peer firm because AI had compressed work that previously took forty hours to a fraction of that time, it was not making a prediction about where the profession was heading. It was describing what had already happened to the economics of that work. The hourly model does not survive the moment a sophisticated client can quantify the AI efficiency gain and ask for a share of it. That moment has arrived.

Ernst & Young has deployed AI-native software delivery pipelines to tens of thousands of consultants, measuring success in productivity gains and delivery speed. The metric — how much faster, how much cheaper — is a Tier 1 measurement applied at enormous scale. The firms measuring AI by speed are running the right race at the wrong distance. Speed is a Tier 1 advantage. It is also the advantage most easily commoditized, because speed is what every system promises and what every competitor will eventually match.

AICPA research published in 2026, surveying more than 1,700 executives globally, found that only 26 percent of firms had made the transition to what the research described as AI-transformed operations — and that the gap between that group and the rest was widening, not closing. The firms pulling ahead were not better resourced or better connected. They had made decisions earlier, learned from them, and built on what they learned. The advantage is not the technology. It is the institutional knowledge that comes from having deployed the technology under real conditions, over multiple cycles, with real clients.

The Credential at the Boundary

The license does not disappear in the hourglass economy. It moves. In the old model, the credential was proof that you could do the production work correctly — that you had accumulated enough knowledge through enough hours of supervised practice to be trusted with complex engagements. The production work and the credential were inseparable, because the production work was how the knowledge behind the credential was built and demonstrated.

In the emerging model, the production work is no longer what the credential certifies. The credential certifies something more precise and more valuable: the judgment to review AI output, identify the items that require professional attention, make the decisions that require domain expertise and professional accountability, and sign the output that carries legal weight. The credential moves to the boundary between the AI system and the output that enters the world. It is less visible in the workflow than it used to be, because it is no longer distributed across hundreds of hours of production supervision. It is concentrated at the point where the output becomes defensible.

This is a more important position than the one the credential occupied before. The credential at the boundary is not a rubber stamp — it is the point of maximum accountability. The output is only as reliable as the judgment applied at that boundary. The professional who occupies that position is the irreplaceable element in the workflow. AI can produce. AI cannot be responsible for what it produces. The responsibility attaches to the signature, and the signature attaches to the credential.

The practices that understand this are building toward it deliberately. They are not asking how to use AI to do what they currently do faster. They are asking how to position the credential at the boundary of an AI-assisted workflow in a way that commands more value, serves more clients, and builds more durable advantage than the production-heavy model that preceded it.

The Intelligent Practice Platform

A new category is emerging at the intersection of professional services and AI — and it does not yet have a widely used name. The shape of it is visible in the practices that have built deliberately, in the products being built by domain experts who understand their workflows deeply enough to encode professional judgment into AI systems, and in the economics that follow when those systems are deployed correctly.

Call it an Intelligent Practice Platform. It is not a software company — it does not sell access to a system and leave the professional judgment to whoever bought the subscription. It is not a traditional professional services firm — it does not price by the hour and grow by hiring more people to do more production work. It is something in between that did not fully exist before the current generation of AI systems made it possible: a practice that encodes professional judgment into AI-augmented workflows, delivers the output at software scale, and maintains the human judgment layer at the boundary where the output carries professional accountability.

The economics of an Intelligent Practice Platform are different from both of its predecessors. The marginal cost of serving one more client is far lower than in a traditional practice, because the production work that used to scale linearly with client count is now handled by AI systems that scale differently. The value per client is higher, because the judgment layer that AI freed up for advisory work is deployed more deeply into each client relationship. The constraint is not hours. It is the quality of the domain logic encoded in the systems, and the professional judgment available to stand behind the output.

This is the destination the implementation playbook has been building toward. Not a practice that uses AI to do what it currently does faster. A practice that has rebuilt what it does around AI, with the professional judgment layer positioned where it creates the most value and the most defensible output.

> *Adding AI to a workflow is not the same as rebuilding the workflow for AI. The practices that build deliberately will look, in three years, like they did the latter. Because they did.*

What the Next Boundary Looks Like

The credential at the boundary of today's AI-assisted workflows is the judgment review — the professional who evaluates AI output and signs the deliverable. That boundary is becoming well understood, and systems are being designed to support it. The next boundary is less well understood, and it will create the next wave of professional opportunity.

As AI systems become more deeply embedded in professional workflows, the question of whether the AI system itself is trustworthy becomes a professional question, not just a technical one. Who certifies that the domain logic encoded in the system is correct? Who attests that the classification rules, the flag logic, and the review workflow produce outputs that a professional can reliably sign? Who provides assurance that the system has not drifted from the standards it was designed to apply?

These are not questions for engineers. They are questions for credentialed professionals who understand both the technical architecture of AI systems and the professional standards those systems are designed to support. The profession that has spent a century developing frameworks for attesting to the reliability of financial information is the natural home for frameworks that attest to the reliability of AI-assisted professional workflows. The practitioners who understand the systems — who built them, who deployed them, who corrected them over multiple cycles of real engagement work — are positioned to define what that attestation looks like.

This is systems assurance — a practice area that does not yet formally exist and that will, within the next decade, be as standard a part of professional services as financial statement audit is today. The practices that are building Intelligent Practice Platforms now are accumulating the domain knowledge and the deployment experience that will make them the natural authors of the systems assurance frameworks that follow. They are not just positioning for the current transition. They are building toward the next one.

The Window

The window of maximum advantage for practitioners who move deliberately is approximately the period between now and when the tools, the frameworks, and the market expectations have normalized enough that every practice has made the transition. That normalization will happen. The profession will adapt. The question is whether your practice is on the leading edge of the adaptation, capturing the margin and building the institutional knowledge that come from moving early, or on the trailing edge, paying the higher cost of a later and more disruptive transition.

The practices that are building now have an advantage that is real and compounding, but it is not permanent. The institutional knowledge built through two years of AI-assisted workflows is a moat — it cannot be purchased or imported, only built. But the window during which that moat is difficult to replicate will eventually close. The practices that wait long enough will find that the transition is still possible but the advantage is gone.

This book was written during that window. The urgency is real. The opportunity is real. The framework, the assessment, the pilot design, the pricing logic — all of it is designed to help you move before the window closes, not to give you more time to think about whether to move.

What survives the transition is not the practices that had the best systems. It is the practices that made the best decisions about when and how to use them — that positioned the credential at the boundary where it creates the most value, that rebuilt the workflow rather than adding AI on top of it, that priced the judgment rather than the production.

The firms that survive will look like software companies that hold CPA licenses. The credential moves to the boundary — not less important, differently positioned. Everything inside that boundary runs on logic. Everything outside it runs on trust.

Vendor Evaluation Scorecard

Use this scorecard during vendor conversations and demos. Score each area 1–3. A total score of 10 or above across all four areas is a strong signal to proceed to pilot. Any area scored 1 is a flag — understand why before deploying on live client work.

1 — Domain Logic

Whose professional judgment is encoded in this system, and is it the right judgment for your workflow?

Question	Score (1–3)	Notes
Who encoded the domain logic? What is their professional background?		
Does the system encode consequences, not just categories?		
Can you show a specific rule the system applies that a general model would not know?		
Domain Logic Score (3–9)		

2 — Failure Behavior

Run a deliberately messy file through the system. Watch what it does with ambiguous items.

Question	Score (1–3)	Notes	
Does the system flag uncertainty visibly, or produce confident wrong answers?			
Can you override a classification? Is the override recorded?			
Does the system learn from corrections, or is it static?			
Failure Behavior Score (3–9)			

3 — Data Architecture

Understand where client data goes and who owns the output before signing anything.

Question	Score (1–3)	Notes	
Where does client data go? What does the data processing agreement say?			
Is client data siloed? Does one client's data influence another's outputs?			
Who owns the output? What does the agreement say about derivative works?			
Is a private/local			

Question	Score (1–3)	Notes
deployment option available or on the roadmap?		
Data Architecture Score (4–12)		

Ask to see the review interface. Not a feature list — the actual screen a reviewer sees on a flagged item.

Question	Score (1–3)	Notes
Show me a flagged item. What does the reviewer see and what are they being asked to decide?		
Does the system provide enough context to make the judgment call without outside research?		
Is the judgment boundary deliberate (by design) or incidental (catch everything it missed)?		
Judgment Boundary Score (3–9)		

Total Score

Result	Interpretation
28–33 — Strong	Proceed to pilot. Low deployment risk.
20–27 — Conditional	Proceed with specific conditions. Address flagged areas before busy season.
10–19 — Caution	Run a limited pilot only. Do not deploy on complex or sensitive client work.
Below 10 — Stop	Do not deploy. The system is not ready for professional services use in your practice.

Workflow Mapping Template

Map each workflow before deciding where to deploy AI. One row per workflow — current tier, target tier, and your notes on bottleneck and first move.

Workflow	Tier (cur. → tgt.)	Bottleneck / First Move
Client intake & docs		
Transaction classification		
Workpaper preparation		
Review & sign-off		
Client communication		
Advisory & planning		
Billing & engagement		

Column Guide

Column	What to Write
Tier (cur. → tgt.)	e.g. 1→2. Where you are today → where you need to be in 12–24 months.
Bottleneck	One sentence. The single thing most limiting this workflow right now.

Column	What to Write
First Move	The smallest action that creates forward momentum. Not the whole solution — just where to start.

90-Day Pilot Checklist

A structured checklist for running a controlled AI pilot before busy season. Work through this in order. Do not skip the preparation phases. The signal quality of the pilot depends on the work done before the first engagement runs through the system.

Phase 1 — Before the Pilot (Days 1–30)

✓	Action	Owner	Done By
	Select the pilot workflow (one workflow only)		
	Select 5–10 pilot clients — representative, not complex or sensitive		
	Define success criteria in writing before the pilot begins		
	Document the current baseline: time per engagement, error rate, review steps		
	Complete the Vendor Evaluation Scorecard (Appendix A) for the selected system		
	Confirm data processing agreement reviewed and acceptable		
	Confirm client data handling meets professional confidentiality obligations		
	Set up the system on a test		

✓	Action	Owner	Done By

environment with non-live data

Staff briefing: what the system does, what the judgment boundary is, how to escalate

Staff walkthrough: live demonstration of the review interface on test data

Establish the override and escalation protocol in writing

Confirm timing: pilot runs at least one full cycle before busy season

Phase 2 — During the Pilot (Days 31–60)

✓	Action	Owner	Done By

Run first pilot engagement. Do not adjust the workflow mid-cycle.

Track: flag volume and type per engagement

Track: reviewer resolution rate (resolved in-system vs. outside research required)

Track: override patterns — what is being corrected and why

Track: time to complete vs. baseline

Hold the workflow steady — no real-time adjustments unless

✓	Action	Owner	Done By
	critical client risk		
	Collect staff feedback in writing after each engagement		
	Run all 5-10 pilot engagements through the full cycle		
	Document every override with reason — this is the dataset for the evaluation		

Phase 3 — Evaluation and Decision (Days 61–90)

✓	Action	Owner	Done By
	Review success criteria against actual results		
	Analyze override patterns: random (reviewer judgment) vs. systematic (system gap)		
	Assess: were any material items missed? Did the review process catch them?		
	Assess: did staff feedback reflect system problems or workflow adjustment needs?		
	Calculate time delta: pilot engagements vs. baseline		
	Make the deployment decision: Expand / Adjust / Stop		
	If Expand: define next client segment and timeline before busy season		

✓	Action	Owner	Done By
	If Adjust: document the specific gap, assign ownership, schedule adjustment cycle		
	If Stop: document the reason. Update the Vendor Evaluation Scorecard.		
	Brief the full team on the decision and the reasoning		
	Update the Workflow Mapping Template (Appendix B) with what you learned		

The pilot is complete when the decision is made and documented. Not when the engagements are done — when the team knows what to do next and why.

Take This Further

The frameworks in this book are designed to be applied, not just read. Download the practitioner worksheets at milairo.com/readers — built for you to run with your team.

The Prioritization Matrix — Worksheet

A fillable PDF version of the Chapter 8 scoring framework. Score your firm's initiatives on impact, risk, and readiness — and sequence the build.

The Three-Tier Self-Assessment

A diagnostic worksheet for mapping your firm's workflows against the three-tier framework. Identify where each workflow currently sits and where it needs to go.

Vendor Evaluation Scorecard — Appendix A

The full scoring template from the book. Four areas, twelve questions, decision guide. Use it in every vendor conversation before committing to a pilot.

Workflow Mapping Template — Appendix B

Map your firm's workflows against the three-tier framework. Current tier, target tier, readiness, bottleneck, first move — one row per workflow.

90-Day Pilot Checklist — Appendix C

The complete pilot checklist from the book. 32 items across three phases — before, during, and evaluation. Print it. Work through it in order.

milairo.com/readers

Scan the code or visit the URL. Free to access.

Victor A. De la Cruz, CPA

Victor A. De la Cruz, CPA, is the founder of Milairo, an AI-native accounting firm building the systems that modern practices and businesses run on. He brings 15+ years of experience in technical accounting and financial reporting, with a career spanning Big 4 public accounting at KPMG and BDO, and senior roles at global companies including Royal Caribbean, Seaboard Marine, and Likewize.

He holds a Master's in Information Systems Auditing & Control from Bowling Green State University and a CPA license from the Puerto Rico Board of Accountancy.

His work sits at the intersection of professional judgment and AI-augmented systems — encoding what practitioners know into software that scales. He is the creator of RealtyLedger, the first intelligent practice platform purpose-built for CPAs serving rental real estate clients, and Paco.tax, an AI-native managed accounting services platform for Puerto Rico businesses.

He is based in Miami, Florida.

milairo.com, realtyledger.ai, linkedin.com/in/vdelacruzcpa

www.ingramcontent.com/pod-product-compliance
Lightning Source LLC
Chambersburg PA
CBHW071456220526
45472CB00003B/819